ABOUT THE AUTHOR

Glen Humphries is a journalist with the *Illawarra Mercury* newspaper and an award-winning beer writer. He's been a journalist for more than 20 years and, in that time has asked the deputy Prime Minister of Australia why we don't switch to driving on the right-hand side of the road, enquired of a pet food company why they don't sell mouse-flavoured cat food and stacks of other far less amusing questions. He used to run an online music magazine called Dragster and now is the man behind the website Beer Is Your Friend (beerisyourfriend.org). Because of his last name he is known by many as "Bear". But his wife and daughter don't call him that, because that would be weird. He has no phobia of clowns, unless one tries to break into his house. He truly doesn't care what sort of beer you drink – even if it's Corona with a wedge of lemon. He is quietly ashamed that he once thought *The Benny Hill Show* was funny. But is quite proud he never thought *Gogglebox* was funny. Not even for a second. He supports the St George Illawarra Dragons even though they give him plenty of reasons not to. He reckons he could take Chuck Norris. Not the Chuck Norris of *Invasion USA*, but the old withered Chuck we know today. He's glad this book is finally finished so he can go back to bludging on the weekends. He doesn't mind ironing but hates cleaning the shower. Come to think of it, he doesn't understand why the shower needs cleaning because soap and water come in contact with it every day. He can't believe you've read this far, but is secretly chuffed that you have. Next time you see him say the code phrase "Scooter Party", that way he'll know you got this far down. If he was able to play a musical instrument, then he'd probably form a band and call it Scooter Party. Maybe their first album would be called "It's the End of the World, Where are the Car Keys?". He's thinking you probably want to get started reading this book you've already paid for.

Also by Glen Humphries

Thousands of stories in the *Illawarra Mercury*

Hundreds of blog posts on Beer Is Your Friend (beerisyourfriend.org)

A piece about hot cross buns going on sale months before Easter in the *Sydney Morning Herald*

Several chapters in the 2012 *Rugby League Almanac*

A stack of unpublished books, including *Kick to Kick – a Diary of a Suburban Footballer*, *Dumbbell – Fumbling Through Fitness* and *Tryhard*, the tale of a season following the often-frustrating St George Illawarra Dragons

The plays *The Old Man of Steel*, set in a retirement home for superheroes, and *668: The Neighbour of the Beast*, about a guy who finds he lives next-door to Satan

THE SLAB

TWENTY-FOUR STORIES OF BEER IN AUSTRALIA

GLEN HUMPHRIES

Beerisyourfriend.org

Aboriginal and Torres Strait Islander people are advised that this publication contains names of people who have passed away.

Copyright Glen Humphries 2017

ISBN: 978-0648032304
The Slab is first published in 2017 by Beer is Your Friend publications
Beerisyourfriend.org
For information or to purchase additional copies email dragstermag@hotmail.com

This book is copyright. All rights reserved. Except for private study, research, criticism or reviews, as permitted under the Copyright Act, no part of this book may be reproduced, stored in a retrieval system, or transmitted in any form or by any means without prior written permission. Enquires can be directed to the author at dragstermag@hotmail.com
Should you happen to quote from this book in your thesis or whatever, it'd be tops if you'd let me know. I reckon it'd be awesome to see my book in someone else's bibliography. By the way, congratulations on reading this far, I reckon no one ever reads this small type on the copyright page. So well done.

National Library of Australia Cataloguing-in-Publication entry

Creator: Humphries, Glen, author
Title: The Slab: 24 stories of beer in Australia/Glen Humphries
9780648032304 (paperback)
Notes: Includes bibliographical references and index
Subjects: Beer-Australia-Anecdotes
Beer-Australia-History
Beer industry-Australia-History

While you have paid money for this book and therefore in the eyes of the law it belongs to you, each and every copy of The Slab is for Kim and Josie.

ACKNOWLEDGEMENTS

You know how, in acknowledgements, you read about how the book was the work of more than one person, and that many others helped out? Well, that's rubbish. No matter how many times I left the laptop unattended I never once saw anyone else sit in front of it and begin writing a chapter for me. It would have been greatly appreciated but it never happened. Because researching and writing a book is a pain in the backside. There were any number of things I would have rather been doing other than reading academic journals or sitting in front of the laptop typing out words. Yes, even cleaning the shower would have been preferable.

That said, some people have provided assistance of the non-writing kind. Most notably my wife, Kim, who helped me with the formatting of the book. And by "helped me" I mean "did it all while I looked on helplessly". I know how to write words, making them look pretty on the page is not my forte. She also borrowed numerous dusty books from the University of Wollongong for me.

Thanks also go to Matt Kirkegaard at the website Brews News for the heads-up about the truth behind the oft-cited story that porter was used to toast the birth of the colony on January 26, 1788.

Thanks to David Hunt – writer of Australian history books *Girt* and *True Girt* for showing an interest in *The Slab* when I mentioned it on Twitter in passing. Okay, so it wasn't really in passing at all. I threw it out there totally deliberately. Anyway, despite being on deadline for his own book, he offered to read a few chapters of *The Slab* and graciously didn't say they were total rubbish. He even passed them onto his publisher. Talk about going above and beyond the call. David, if loads of other authors now contact you on Twitter about their book, I do apologise.

Thanks to David as well as John Birmingham and James Smith for providing cover blurbs for *The Slab*, thereby making it look a bit more like a proper book.

To Jack Marx, from whom I stole the idea of writing an introduction for each chapter. It came from his wonderful book *Australian Tragic*. It offers conclusive proof that history can be fascinating.

Kate Shepherd designed the cover but declined the offer of giving herself credit for it on the back. But she can't stop me from doing that here – thanks Kate.

Thanks goes to beer, without which this book simply wouldn't exist and I'd have to find a much less enjoyable hobby (by which I mean drinking beer. Writing books isn't a hobby – it's work).

Thanks also go to my parents, without whom none of me would have been possible. And to my aunt Barbara, who knew I would write a book a long, long time before I did. Sorry it took so long. And sorry you're not around to see it.

Lastly but no means leastly, thanks to you, the reader. I'm genuinely appreciative that you chose to spend some of your hard-earned money to buy this book and I did the best I could to try and make it entertaining for you.

"Australians have never been quite the nation of boozers they imagine themselves to be."

Donald Horne
The Lucky Country (1964)

CONTENTS

A Note to the reader

Page 1

Introduction

Jeez, We Aussies Love a Beer, Don't We?

Page 5

1 Captain Cook's attempt at BYO

Page 15

2 First Beers and the Big Party

Page 21

3 Australia's First Hanging

Page 33

4 Battle of our First Brewers

Page 39

5 Bennelong and James Squire

Page 49

6 Government Becomes a Brewer

Page 59

7 Coopers – the Original Craft Brewer

Page 67

8 The Jailing of Edmund Resch

Page 73

9 Fosters – It's American for Beer?

Page 81

10 State-Based Drinking

Page 87

11 The Capital With No Beer

Page 95

12 The Battle of Central Station

Page 101

13 Banning Booze in Australia

Page 111

14 Six O'Clock Closing

Page 121

15 The Darwin Rebellion

Page 131

16 Mining Black Gold From Brewer's Yeast

Page 137

17 What Are All The Xs For?

Page 143

18 The Darwin Stubby

Page 149

19 Breathe Easy with RBT

Page 157

20 Drinking for Australia

Page 165

21 Alan Bond: How to Lose Money and Alienate Drinkers

Page 171

22 The Family Fights Back

Page 179

23 An Army of Talking Boony Dolls

Page 183

24 What is Australia's Most Expensive Beer?

Page 191

Bibliography

Page 199

Index
Page 211

A NOTE TO THE READER

"Australian history was fascinating. And it was bloody funny."
David Hunt, Girt

Yes, it is David, yes it is. But this fact was something I really only discovered while researching and writing *The Slab*. Like most people of my vintage, the amount of Australian history I learned in high school was exactly zero. I studied both modern and ancient history all the way to Year 12 and the very country in which the classroom I was sitting in was located never rated a mention. Not even in the modern history periods where we learned about World War I – which was taught from a very European perspective. And thus I left school knowing the name of the man who shot Franz Ferdinand and thereby started World War I (Gavrilo Princip – didn't even have to Google it. Why my brain chooses to hang onto that piece of information I will never know) but not the name of our first Prime Minister. That, ashamed as I am to say it, I learned from a TV ad that aired several years ago designed to embarrass clueless dolts like myself.

I understand the situation regarding teaching our own history in high school has changed – and a very good thing it is too. I just hope the school history curriculum isn't like school curriculums everywhere else, which seem to be based on one concept – "okay, let's work out which are the most boring parts of this subject and then that's what we'll teach". Because, as Mr Hunt states above, the Australian story is a fascinating one. It's full of great stories – and some of them involve beer or other forms of alcohol. That includes the tale of the rioting soldiers in World War I, the NSW politician whose actions essentially led to a half-century of the pubs closing at 6pm, the Australian city where alcohol was banned before the first building was constructed and even the fact the First Fleet's departure may have been delayed by a day due to sailors being too hungover to sail.

This book – and my interest in Australian history – actually started because of beer. I'm a self-confessed beer geek and, as I got more deeply fascinated by it, I started reading books about the subject. Time and again, those books would make some small reference to an event in Australia's past – the Central Station riot, the Darwin Rebellion, a drunken orgy that happened soon after the First Fleet's arrival. It'd be just a few lines, but they would stop me in my tracks and I'd talk to the author in my head – "Hold your horses guy, I want to hear more about that."

But obviously they never heard me. So I had to go find out the full story myself. That involved reading a lot of Australian history books. Soon enough I got into the habit of going straight to the index and looking for "beer" before reading the whole book. Initially, there were only a handful of such tales I looked at and I used them to write a week-long series of pieces for my blog Beer Is Your Friend (go check it out at beerisyourfriend.org. I'll still be here when you get back) called History in a Bottle.

And yet, I kept finding more stories. I kept thinking to myself "I wish someone would write a book about these stories, because I'd like to read it". I'm sure that's served as the inspiration for many a book – cursing an apparent gap in the book market and deciding to write something to fill it up. Which leads me – and you – to *The Slab*; Spakfilla aimed at patching up a long overlooked section of Australian history.

If you're like me, it may seem more than a little surprising that no one has written a book dedicated to Australian history and beer. After all, we love to think that beer is such an important part of our culture that it seems a no-brainer that a book is warranted. Or maybe publishers figure we're too busy drinking the stuff to read about it. Who knows?

Anyway, there are two aims with *The Slab* – to be historically accurate and to be interesting. In reference to that first point, I have spent quite a bit of time reading and researching these stories. In the process I've found history is not always as black and white as you expect. Some of it is very much open to interpretation and, frustratingly, we may never know what actually happened. I've tried to base each chapter on the most accurate information – or interpretations – I could find. Everything in this book may not be 100 per cent accurate but it's as accurate as I could make it. Keep in mind I'm not a historian, I'm just some guy who sat down and read a lot of stuff and then wrote about it as best he could.

And that idea about writing leads me to that second aim – to be interesting. I didn't want *The Slab* to be a dry, factual read; instead I wanted it to be fun. Serious books about beer strike me as a bit oxymoronic. It's beer, it's supposed to be fun. And history can be fun too. So where it's appropriate I've injected some humour to make things more entertaining and help make some of these great stories come to life.

History is full of great stories and some of the best live at the margins. They're the stories of what may seem like small moments involving ordinary people rather than kings or prime ministers. They're those stories that only get touched on in most history books, where the author is too busy dealing with the "important" stuff to pay much attention to what is going on near the sidelines. So I hope people will find a number of stories here that they've never heard before.

If I happen to pique your interest with one of these tales and you want to know a bit more yourself, there's an extensive bibliography at the back to help you find out where to go next. Anyway, I hope you enjoy reading this as much as I enjoyed researching it.

Glen Humphries
Wollongong
November 2016

INTRODUCTION
JEEZ, US AUSSIES LOVE A BEER, DON'T WE?

Ahhh, beer. It's our national drink, isn't it? We drink it at the pub, at home, at a barbecue, at parties, at a range of sporting events, after we've done some manual labour that could range from laying a concrete slab to replacing a light bulb. Pretty much anywhere we can get away with it ("Sorry Father, I thought if you allowed the altar wine in church, then it'd be alright if I cracked open a beer").

If some bloke says he doesn't drink beer, well, we look at him a bit differently. Hey, this is Australia, mate. We drink beer here, so get used to it. In fact, we drink more beer here in Australia than anywhere else. It was like that from the moment the convicts landed. It's always been like that and it always will be.

Well, actually, my friend, it hasn't always been like that at all. For most of the time since the convicts rocked up we've been pretty average when it comes to beer drinking — with the exception of a decade or two. In fact, give it a couple of years and beer won't even be the country's most popular drink any more …

Us Australians love to think of ourselves as a nation that has forever been one of the big beer drinkers. One that ranks in the top five beer-drinking nations on Earth every single time whoever it is compiles one of those lists.

We know Bob Hawke more for his record-setting talents with a yard of ale than for anything he did in his eight years leading the country. The man himself acknowledged this in his autobiography – "This feat was to endear me to some of my fellow Australians more than anything else I ever achieved". Just dwell on that for a second – he was the leader of the country for eight years and he had to resign himself to be well-known for success at drinking beer from a glass that these days is only ever used at 21st birthday parties.

When Hawkey skulls a beer at the cricket – which he has done at least three times according to YouTube – we figure it can't get more "Aussie" than that. Except when he does it at the urging of a crowd of people dressed up like Richie Benaud – YouTube again. These days, other Australian politicians know that, if they want to be more popular, they make sure they stage at least one media opp in a pub so they can be seen drinking a beer. And a proper beer, out of a schooner glass – Prime Minister Tony Abbott copped a bit when he was seen drinking a middy. Come on, man, go big or go home.

And, David Boon, my God do we love David Boon. But we love him more for being an opener of beers than an opener of the batting order. We remember him most for drinking a crapload of beers on the flight from Australia to England (though, to be fair, the man himself has never admitted to it). Later, a miniature talking version of Boony helped Carlton and United sell a truckload of VB slabs (even though it wasn't actually Boony's voice drinkers heard). We love him so much he appears in three separate chapters of this book. And, while there seem to be conflicting schools of thought on whether his nickname is spelt "Boony" or "Boonie", I've gone with the former throughout *The Slab*. For no reason other than I think it looks much better in print.

Yep, us Aussies, jeez we love a beer. Beer is tops, right?

But here's the thing. This idea we have that we're a nation of beer lovers and have always been like that? It's a con – a fib we've let ourselves believe because, for some strange reason, we think it's great to be seen as a nation of drunks. Aside from a decade or two in the 20th century we've never been one for knocking back slabs of beer (sure, there was a decade or two after the First Fleet's arrival when a lot of people seemed to be tanked a lot of the time, but that was on spirits, not beer). And we haven't been among the world's biggest beer-drinking countries for ages.

While the story goes that Governor Arthur Phillip toasted the health of the colony of Sydney with a dark beer called porter on January 26, 1788 – and as we shall see in Chapter Two, that seems doubtful – beer wasn't that big a deal in the early decades of the colony. The drink of choice was wine or rum, because it travelled so much better than beer. The fact that, on a volume basis, rum allowed more people to get drunk than beer didn't hurt either. Spirits, to a large degree, were also used as a surrogate currency in the colony's early days.

As for beer, despite the work of James Squire and John Boston – the actual people and not the companies that co-opted their names even though they had no actual link to them – it was bloody hot in Australia. That may be great beer-drinking weather but it's crap beer-making weather, especially when refrigeration was yet to be invented.

"The problem involved in supplying adequate quantities of drinkable beer were less easily solved," wrote academic AE Dingle of the early colonial days in his excellent academic paper 'The Truly Magnificent Thirst' (yes, academics write about beer). "Beer is a bulky commodity relative to its value and, until recently, has tended to deteriorate rapidly with age."

Still, some brewers persevered and, by the early 1800s, there were 10 breweries in Sydney and regional ones were popping up all over the place. But the quality was very hit and miss. By the 1830s, according to statistics from Dingle's paper, beer drinking rates in NSW were about 19 litres per person per year. Due to the limited production of beer across the country, he takes an educated guess that the level of beer drinking have remained around that mark for most of the 1800s. Hard to drink lots of beer if no-one is making much of it. And so spirits and wines tend to remain the intoxicant of choice around this time. Though Melbourne went through a phase in the 1840s when they were totally mad for champagne, according to writer Robyn Annear. As the city grew, land lots were auctioned off at what were tagged "champagne lunches", because there was heaps of free booze available.

Governor Gipps from Sydney paid a visit in 1842 and found "the whole country for miles, almost for hundreds of miles, round Melbourne is strewed to this day with champagne bottles".

According to Annear, "legend has it than cairns of them marked the boundaries of the town, and the roadsides along (present day) Wellington Parade and over the Eastern Hill to Fitzroy bristled with dead marines".

However, back to the subject of beer. In his essay 'A New Drink for Young Australia', Brett J Stubbs said it was hardly surprising the heavy ales made here at the time weren't too flash.

"Early Australian brewers could not have been expected to produce good quality local beers. They were heavily handicapped by a warm climate and by generally inferior water supplies. In addition their equipment was primitive, raw materials (malt and hops) were often inferior, and highly skilled brewers were unavailable."

That drinking figure of 19 litres per person quoted by Dingle more than doubles by the 1890s to about 50 litres per capita. This roughly coincided with better scientific brewing techniques - which Stubbs said helped brewers get rid of the so-called "colonial twang" – and the use of refrigeration.

This was also around the time lager was introduced; a more refreshing beer for the warmer climate than the heavier ales of Britain that had been proffered to the Australian drinker. Stubbs said it took 20-odd years for it to really take hold – some felt that stinking hot Australian weather be damned, we should stick to the thick dark ale of our British roots – but take hold it did.

By the way, that average of 50 litres per person? In case you think that's a lot, it was substantially below the 136 litres the average British person was putting away each year at the same time.

With more consistent figures available for the 20th century, the amount of beer drunk in Australia each year is surprisingly stable – it stayed around about that 50-litre mark through to the 1930s. This period includes the introduction of six o'clock closing in 1916, which clearly did not have the intended effect of reducing anyone's drinking. What did have an effect was the Great

Depression in the late 1920s - the rates dropped to 30 litres a year for almost a decade. Hard to buy a beer when you've got no money. Or a job.

Then World War II comes along and, despite a lot of the men of beer-drinking age being overseas at war, the per capita drinking volume increased. Must have been all those American soldiers coming over here drinking our beer and stealing our women. By the end of the war the drinking rates hit 72 litres per capita. And then it kept going up and up, reaching 110 litres by the mid-1950s – the tail-end of the six o'clock swill.

And still it went up – 120 litres in 1969, 130 in 1972 and 142 in 1974. Right about this time, as academic Diane Kirkby points out, was when social commentators started writing about Australian culture and society. "With some irony, they captured the essence of an Australian drinking culture that was partly a result of past history but was also indicative of a moment of transition," Kirkby said.

And with that much beer being poured down the necks of Australians, it would have been hard for them not to comment on our drinking habits. But they went a bit too far and suggested it had always been that way. "It was a misconception to think drunkenness was the national character," Kirkby wrote.

Things began to change in the late 1970s, and for a number of reasons. It was the tail-end of a long period of prosperity in Australia, the increasing number of migrants entering the country began to change the culture of the country and there was a growing desire for co-ed drinking spaces rather than the bar being blokes-only while women were stuck in the "ladies lounge".

These and other factors conspired to bring down the amount of beer we drank. The Australian Bureau of Statistics reports a steady decline in beer-drinking from the 1970s through to today.

"Apparent consumption of pure alcohol from beer rose strongly in the decade following World War II, followed by a period of slower growth. Apparent consumption of beer peaked in 1973-74 and 1974-75 at an average of 9.2 litres of pure alcohol [which is distinct from volume of beer, hence the smaller number] per person aged 15 years and over. Since then, the prevalence of beer has decreased markedly, reaching 4.6 litres of pure alcohol per person in 2004-05 and remaining at this level in the following years. This is half that of the peak in the mid-1970s, and the lowest since 1947-48."

The "pure alcohol" measure can be a bit confusing. How many litres of beer were we drinking? The ABS states the post-war peak was in the mid-1970s when beer consumption was around 190 litres per person aged 15 years and over. By 2008-09 that had dropped to 107, the lowest since 1947-48.

On a graph from the ABS showing wine and drinking rates over time, from the 1970s onwards the line for beer is moving steadily downhill, while the lines for wine and spirits steadily move upwards. In 2015, Louise Gates from the bureau said beer made up 41 per cent of all alcohol consumed, compared to 75 per cent 50 years ago. That's less than half – hardly sounds like our national drink does it?

There's a good chance it won't be our favourite drink for much longer either. Wine makes up 37.5 per cent and – if the current trend of beer falling and wine drinking rising keeps on going – in a few years it will overtake beer as the most popular alcoholic beverage in Australia. Then it will be more accurate to say we're a nation of wine drinkers, rather than beer drinkers.

And our world ranking when it comes to beer? Sorry to say, that seems a bit of a myth too. By mega-brewer Kirin's calculations in 2012, we're not in the top five. Top 10? Nope. On a per capita basis, we're 11th - three spots south of our 2011 ranking. Above us are some countries no one ever thinks of when the topic of beer-drinking nations comes up. Did you ever think the Finns were the type to murder a beer? Nope? Well, Finland is ahead of us in the beer-drinking stakes, according to Kirin. So is Venezuela. Yes, Venezuela.

When you look at the Kirin figures for the total volume of beer consumed, leaving out any per capita calculations, we're even lower on the list. As of 2012, we were ranked 24th in the world, behind the likes of Japan (seventh), Vietnam (12th), Nigeria (19th) and Argentina (23rd).

So, why do we have this idea that we're a nation of beer drinkers when, for great swathes of our history, it is clearly not true? I'm blaming those social commentators in the 1960s. It was a period of navel-gazing, where we stopped to have a good look at ourselves for the first time. And what those commentators saw was a lot of beer being drunk. So they wrote about it – and not in a positive light I may add. But perhaps the larrikin streak that ran through Australia at the time took some perverse pride in being a nation of pissheads ("hey, at least we're really good at something") and latched onto that image of ourselves.

We're good at getting the wrong idea about ourselves. Take the phrase "The lucky country"- we've taken that to mean that Australia is tops. But that's not what it means at all – it was a bit of a backhander from author and, yes, social commentator, Donald

Horne. He was saying we just stumbled into things by dumb luck rather than any genuine effort on our part. Kind of like the guy who inherits his wealth from his dad but tries to tell himself he made it himself.

So, that image of us being a nation of boozers, over time it took hold and became set in concrete until it just became an accepted fact of Australian life. Even though it wasn't a "fact" at all. And, as the internet has shown time and time again, once people start believing something is true, it can be an uphill climb to reverse that ("Look, my mind's made up. Stop confusing me with facts!").

It's a great mystery to me as to why on Earth we thought buying into this image of ourselves as borderline alcoholics was a good thing. It's another mystery as to why we continue to believe in it. If this image of Australia was a person, they'd be embarrassing. They'd be the one arriving at the party slurring their words, the one who would corner people and bore them senseless with the incoherent crap coming out their mouths, who would think they're being charming when they're actually being obnoxious, who would get in a fight with another guest in the front yard, be asked to leave, vomit in someone's hedge on the way home and wake up the next day still wearing the same clothes from the night before.

If this image of Australia was a person, you'd do your best to avoid them. If they moved in next-door to you, then you'd start looking at real estate websites to find a new house. If they were a workmate you'd stop going to the work Christmas party.

But the image just isn't true. Fortunately.

But if you want to continue to believe that being drunk is part of our national character, and you want to keep conforming to an image of Australia that no longer exists, then be advised that it says more about you than the country. And also, don't throw up in my front yard on your way home.

ONE

CAPTAIN COOK'S ATTEMPT AT BYO

When it comes to beer, Australia's story starts with Captain James Cook – or Lieutenant James Cook as he was known at the time he visited our shores. Yes, there may be a chance Spaniard Luis Vaz de Torres might have had a few barrels when, in 1606, he sailed through the strait which now bears his name. Captain John Brooks may have had some beer on board when he skirted the Western Australian coast in 1622, ages before Cook arrived.

William Dampier could have had some on his ship, the Cygnet, when he landed on the coast of our western side in 1688. The French are stereotypically known for their wine, but maybe their sailor Louis-Antoine de Bougainville had some beer with him when he came within sight of the Great Barrier Reef in 1767.

Yes, they were all in the neighbourhood long before Jimmy C, but let us not complicate things. For our purpose – and indeed for history's – James Cook was the white man who discovered Australia (though there were obviously more than a few Aboriginal people who were aware of its existence long before him – but it's highly doubtful they were brewing beer, which what concerns us in this book).

And that white man had beer on the Endeavour – for part of the voyage at least. The crew ran through it pretty quickly, which led some to think they were truly drunken sailors. But there's a bit more to it than that. And one of the key reasons Cook had it on board turned out to be completely wrong ...

These days, if we're going on a round-the-world cruise, we want to do it in a great big ship. But they didn't do things that way back in the days of James Cook. When you look at Cook's journey on the Endeavour two things are immediately striking – how bloody long the trip was and how bloody small the Endeavour was.

We tend to think of Cook's trip having everything to do with discovering Australia and nothing to do with anything else. But he had other duties, some of which – like observing the transit of Venus – took precedence over looking for some great hunk of land at the bottom of the world. And, once he found Australia, we tend to forget Cook had to return home. So he sailed all the way around the world on a voyage that took him about four years – from 1768-1771. Imagine if you had a job that took you away from home for FOUR years.

He made that four-year trip on a tiny, bath-toy of a ship. Looking at the dimensions of the Endeavour – about 29 metres long and nine metres wide – doesn't really send the message about how small it really was. But I reckon this does – based on those measurements, Cook sailed for four years around the world in a ship that you could fit in an Olympic swimming pool. And still have about 20 metres in length to spare. Just think about that next time you're at your suburban swimming pool.

In that tiny ship Cook had to fit all the crew and the supplies he needed. When he left Britain, the ship's holds included all sorts of supplies. Among the pork, beef, flour, sauerkraut and raisins, were 250 barrels of beer. Which seems a substantial amount at first, and something that would take up a lot of space in the ship.

Cook's diary mentions taking on supplies of beer on August 16 and 25, 1768, setting sail on the latter date. With space at a premium it was perhaps a good thing the 90-odd people on board the Endeavour managed to neck most of the beer after being at sea for just on a month. By September 27, Cook wrote "served Wine to the ship's company, the beer being all expended but 2 casks, which I intend to keep some time longer, as the whole has proved very good to the last cask."

At first glance, it seems like the crew of the Endeavour were gargantuan pissheads. After all, they got through 248 of the 250 barrels of beer in a little over 30 days. Not even the passengers on Fairstar the Funship get through that much beer that quickly.

But Cook doesn't seem to give any indication of how big those barrels were; in fact in descriptions of the beer's housing, the words "barrels" and "casks" are used interchangeably. If we use the internet as a source (and, as we know the internet is never ever wrong) a barrel would hold about 136 litres. So if the Endeavour was carrying barrels it had a whopping 34,000 litres of beer on board, which I think we can agree seems a bit much for what ended up being only be a month's supply.

If we take the figure of 96 crew on board (which some sources mention) that means, between setting sail and September 27, they drank five barrels a day. That's a total of 680 litres each day – or seven litres per person per day. Which in turn equates to about a case of beer every day. I don't care how much of a salty old sea dog you are, there's no way you're getting through that much beer every day. For a month and a half. No matter how bad the onboard entertainment options are.

But what if they were casks rather than barrels? Again relying on the infallible internet, a cask could carry about 41 litres. So, those

96 crew drinking five casks a day means each one of them drank about two litres a day. Which seems much more reasonable and in keeping with what seemed to be the average daily beer ration for a sailor at that time, which was about three litres in today's measure. It should be said what we're talking about is "small beer", which is low in alcohol. The small beer did not so much serve as an intoxicant but rather a replacement for fresh water, which was hard to store on a ship for long periods at sea.

Which isn't to say the crew on the Endeavour were all for the responsible service of alcohol and knew when they'd had enough. As well as that beer ration, the sailors got into the rum. There are several references in Cook's diary to crew members getting absolutely stonkered. When the Endeavour was docked at Rio de Janeiro, the ship's quartermaster Robert Anderson got flogged for, well, being extremely flogged. John Reading, the guy who was supposed to flog him, was himself too pissed to do the job, so he got whipped too. It wouldn't be the last time Reading got drunk. He actually died of alcohol poisoning while on board the Endeavour when he drank half a bottle of rum all in one go.

Cook's clerk Richard Orton also got into some strife on board. One night he got so smashed that, after he went to sleep, someone cut off all his clothes and slashed parts of his ears – and the man did not wake up. You have to be pretty pissed not to realise when someone is cutting into you – that's alcohol as anaesthetic.

Aside from facilitating amateur ear surgery, why was Cook carrying beer at all? Keep in mind he also had 44 barrels of brandy and 17 barrels of rum on board as well. Well, the beer (and the other alcohol) was there partially because sailing for months on end can be pretty boring and you want to keep sailors from getting cranky and punching each other. Or whatever it was 18th century sailors did when they got cranky – going all van Gogh on each other and slashing ears seems a possibility.

The beer, and not the other forms of alcohol, was on board for another purpose. Cook was a proponent of the belief at the time that beer helped to combat scurvy. As an added measure, he was also carrying wort (unfermented beer) and malt. The British Navy had been losing quite a few sailors from scurvy at the time and so they were keen to find a cure. The sailors were perhaps even more keen, because there were plenty of better ways to die than developing scurvy. It starts with fatigue, followed by spots on the skin. Then your gums get spongy so your teeth fall out. And then you start bleeding from your nose while previously healed wounds decide to open up and bleed too. After a while, you die. So the sailors said, "we'll have less of that, if you please".

According to Queensland academic Brett J Stubbs, the reason the navy thought beer and malt could ward off scurvy was because symptoms would tend to show up after a month at sea - which is when the beer ran out. But they were wrong – it was ascorbic acid or vitamin C that stopped people getting scurvy.

"With our present understanding of the cause of the disease however," Stubbs wrote in a paper on the subject, "we would recognise that the depletion of the sea stock of beer would coincide with the depletion of bodily reserves of ascorbic acid in the absence of a dietary source."

During the voyage to Australia, Cook was issued with instructions to mix up malt with water, let it stand for several hours and give each person a litre a day. He managed to ward off scurvy on his first voyage and then the next two at the helm of The Endeavour, a feat which saw him lauded by many. Which was good, until you realise Cook likely had no idea exactly what he was doing that was warding off scurvy. As well as trying the malty water, Cook gave a load of other things a crack, as a ridiculously long list included in Stubbs' paper indicates;

"Close attention to cleanliness on board the ship; by maintaining a plentiful supply of fresh water; by procuring fresh food wherever possible; and by carrying and using a variety of substances which had known or suspected antiscorbutic properties. These substances included such things as sauerkraut, salted cabbage, portable broth (a soup, prepared from cattle offal and flavoured with salt and vegetables, then evaporated to hard cakes), salep (a powder made from dried orchid roots), mustard, marmalade of carrots, rob of lemon and orange (their juice evaporated to a syrup) and malt and inspissated juice of wort and beer."

I think we can agree that's a real grab-bag of options and there's no way of knowing what was effective and what wasn't. One thing's for sure, the beer wasn't doing anything in terms of stopping scurvy. Nor the wort or malt. Several outbreaks of scurvy occurred on other ships in the 1790s, despite the administration of malt or beer and, by 1790 the navy had given up it and recommended using lemon juice – which would certainly have worked. And taken up far less room on board that all those casks of beer and wort.

While beer was totally useless when it came to preventing scurvy, it was quite handy for other uses. Like, getting drunk, mainly. So it's not really all that much of a surprise that beer turns up fairly soon after a group of ships known as the First Fleet arrive. But perhaps not quite as soon as we've been led to believe.

TWO

FIRST BEERS AND THE BIG PARTY

Australians love a party, so the story goes. The louder the better — if at least one neighbour doesn't get angry about the noise and call the cops then you weren't trying hard enough. So I've heard — I'm usually the cranky neighbour crying out in exasperation "Dear God, don't they know some of us are trying to sleep?"

So with that in mind, it's not really a surprise that so many of us love the idea that the founding of Australia kicked off with a drunken orgy in the vicinity of Circular Quay way back in 1788, about a week after the First Fleet arrived. The female convicts were unloaded onto Australian soil and then the party started.

But if you think about it for a minute, it's not really a great way to start a nation — because surely there would have been a number of females not at all willing to be a part of this party. Which means people like the idea of the country effectively being founded on sexual assault.

If this wild party actually did happen, that is.

There's something else we've been told happened around this time, that may actually not be true — the idea that Arthur Phillip and his mates cracked open a few beers as soon as they set foot on the shore of Sydney Harbour. Australia was toasted with a beer? Sounds like a great story. If it's true …

Okay, so there were two beer-related events surrounding the First Fleet that are either dubious or perhaps overstated. But before we get there allow me to make a few digressions about the founding of this country. Because it all seems more than a little weird.

Captain Cook "discovered" Australia in 1770 – even though any number of other people found it before him. Including the people actually living *in* the country at the time. When he returned home botanist Joseph Banks stole the limelight and talked up this wonderful place. In fact, it was he who put the thought into the higher-ups heads that Australia could totally support a colony. So, in 1788, Captain Arthur Phillip arrived with the First Fleet full of people those in Britain did not like very much at all and were dead keen to see the back of. Even if the door did hit their arses on the way out.

But here's the weird thing. There were 18 years between Cook claiming Australia for Britain and the First Fleet arriving to set up a prison. You know how many times the British sent a ship or two our way in those intervening 18 years, just to suss things out? Zero. Yep, they stuck a flag in it, mapped it and then forgot all about it – until they decided they needed somewhere to chuck their criminals now that America wasn't having any of that and leaving them on ships in the Thames wasn't really working.

Even then did they think, "hey, if we're going to send a load of people to this land in the middle of nowheresville, perhaps we should do a little research on the place first"? No, they did not. One might get the impression that they didn't care all that much about what would happen to those on the First Fleet once they arrived. Out of sight, out of mind, as they say – and it's hard to get more "out of sight" than at the other end of the world.

You wouldn't take one look at a house and then decide to buy it 18 years later without at least a second look, would you? Well, you would if you were a moron but you bought this book so clearly you have some smarts about you. So you're not going to buy a house that way, and yet the English decided to settle a whole country without so much as a second glance. Clearly we were just some investment property the buyers never intended on living in themselves.

This total lack of research became blindingly obvious when the First Fleet arrived in January 1788 and was greeted by the Australian summer – that time of year that causes grass to die and massive cracks to open up on cricket pitches that commentators can stick their keys into. Arriving at Botany Bay they must surely have thought Joseph Banks had been taking the piss when he gave the place a favourable review ("close to water. Lots of plants. Friendly neighbours. Five stars!"). Cook can shoulder a bit of the blame, he thought there was so much growing in the soil that he called the place *Botany* Bay.

But Banks and Cook saw the land in April, didn't they? In the middle of autumn, where the sun opts not to scorch everything to a cinder and the earth's had a bit of rain. Britain knew so little about the country they'd just sent boatloads of people to that it didn't even seem to think the weather wouldn't always be like it was on the 10 or so days Cook hung around.

The First Fleet arrived in Australia on January 19 – yep, not January 26 like you thought. One by one the ships rocked up at Botany Bay and the crew said to themselves, "This place is crap. Banks was so taking the piss". Three days later, Arthur Phillip took a small party slightly north, to check out some inlet called Port Jackson that Cook had noted but sailed past. As oversights go it was a pretty big one on Cook's part, for that inlet turned out to be Sydney Harbour, or as Arthur Phillip said when they rowed past the heads, "Holy crap, this place is fully sick!". Okay, so he didn't say those exact words but the sentiment was the same.

Phillip got word to the rest of the fleet that they'd be setting up shop in the new harbour he'd just found. But as they were preparing to leave, the weirdness surrounding the settling of Australia continued. In the waters outside Botany Bay were two ships, soon to be identified as the expedition of the Comte de la Perouse, from France, who had been exploring the Pacific for three years. By some jaw-dropping coincidence, these two fleets had travelled halfway around the world and managed to arrive at Botany Bay at the same time. As it was, the French ships entering Botany Bay literally passed the last of the First Fleet leaving the very same bay.

But if the aim was to keep cool as they sailed out of Botany Bay, the First Fleet was spectacularly unsuccessful, according to William Cropton Sever, captain of the Lady Penrhyn. Several ships managed to crash into each other while trying to exit the bay. Might I suggest, for added amusement, you play the theme to *The Benny Hill Show* in your head as you read this passage;

"Charlotte was once in the most imminent danger of being on the rocks. The Friendship and Prince of Wales… came foul of each other … the Friendship carried away her jib boom and The Prince of Wales has her mainsail and main topmast staysail rent in pieces by the Friendship's yard. The Charlotte also afterwards ran foul of the Friendship and carried away a great deal of the carved work for her [Charlotte's] stern and it was with the greatest difficulty

our ship avoided the same fate…"

When the ships all arrived at Sydney Cove, in the harbour, they anchored that night. The next morning, January 26, they got busy on the shore. To mark the occasion – even though, technically, they'd actually arrived in Australia a good seven days earlier – Phillip and several others hoisted the British flag, drank a toast to the King and his family, and then a second to the health of the colony. Marines who were present then sent a volley of fire skyward. And thus was the first Australia Day (except it wasn't – it seems Phillip saw the nation's symbolic birth in the reading out of the proclamation of the colony and his governorship which happened on February 4).

So now, let's get to the part about beer. The popular telling of this story of Arthur and his men standing around the flag and offering up toasts says they were doing it with cups of porter. On the surface that does seem to make some sense; porter was a popular style of beer in Britain at the time. But, here's the thing, there doesn't seem to be any contemporary record of that event at Sydney Cove where porter is mentioned. In fact, no diary, letter or other contemporary document I've seen actually names what they were drinking around the flagpole. The diary of Captain Philip Gidley King, which does mention people drinking porter, could be the origin of this claim – so it's a pity he mentions the porter-drinking happening a full seven days early than the January 26 flag-raising at Sydney Cove.

On January 19, King was at Botany Bay on the HMS Supply. In his diary he wrote that a number of them climbed into small boats and explored a nearby river and inlets around the bay. About that afternoon he writes, "we went ashore and ate our salt beef and in a glass of porter drank [to] the health of our friends in England".

Then King stays at Botany Bay while Governor Phillip goes north to check out Port Jackson – aka Sydney Harbour. Phillip returns on the 23rd and says "we're moving" and so King et al sail north to Port Jackson. There, on the morning of January 26, King writes that "the English colours were displayed onshore and possession was taken for His Majesty whose health, with the Queen's, Prince of Wales and success to the colony was drank, a feu de joie was fired by a party of marines and the whole gave three cheers which was returned by the Supply."

But no mention of porter at Sydney Cove at all. They definitely toasted the colony with *something*; could have been porter. Could have been wine, rum, brandy, madeira or any other spirit. There just doesn't seem to be any evidence of exactly what they drank around the flag on the morning of January 26, 1788.

Though, the idea that the country was founded over a few beers will tend to appeal to people, who may then point to this moment and say "see? Australians love beer so much it was the first thing they drank when they got here." Which is certainly true – by King's own words, he drank beer on the shore at Botany Bay. And, if you think about it, that makes more sense. If you've just been on a bloody long sea voyage and you reach your destination, you'll likely have a drink to celebrate immediately. The guys on the First Fleet weren't thinking, "hang on, we should hold off on drinking anything on shore here at Botany Bay. You know, just in case the Governor gets it into his head that we have to move".

Even before setting foot on dry land at Botany Bay, there was a beer connection with the First Fleet. It was among the rations for both sailor and convict – even on the prison hulks in the Thames before the First Fleet sailed prisoners got about a litre of "small beer". This low-alcohol brew was more a replacement for water than a means of getting wrecked.

There was also beer being brewed on the First Fleet ships too. Arthur Bowes Smyth, the ship's doctor on board the convict transport Lady Penrhyn mentions in his diary that he was brewing spruce beer. He even includes the recipe (complete with random capitalisation) – "take 10 gallons of water, lukewarm, eight pounds of molasses (or treacle), Six Table spoonfulls of Essence of Spruce, One pint of Yeast, Stir it well together – it will be fit for bottling in a week & for drinking in a week after". Despite sounding quite unappetising, that spruce beer would have been very advantageous for the good doctor's health – the spruce contains vitamin C, crucial in warding off scurvy.

There is another story about these early days that Australians love. While it is unlikely that beer played much of a role in the proceedings, it is too good a tale to leave untold. It's the tale that there was a wild party – or orgy, take your pick – on the shore near what is now Circular Quay two weeks after the arrival at Sydney Cove. So the tale goes, the male convicts had already been let off the ships and when the women came ashore on February 6 everyone went crazy and let their hair down in a riot of sex and drinking after months at sea. That's a great story about the founding of the nation; that we marked it with a massive blow-out. It drew me in the first time I read about it.

But if you think about what this wild party/orgy would have entailed it doesn't seem that great. If this event did happen, it would have probably involved some non-consensual sex – what we'd consider today as rape or sexual assault. Hardly the sort of thing you'd want to boast as forming the foundations of the country. The fact we started out as a bunch of convicts is bad enough. Though there are those historians who state the women would have been as willing as the men to get down and dirty. But *all* of the women?

In her book, *The Colony – A History of Early Sydney*, Grace Karskens puts forward the theory that the orgy never happened because the evidence just isn't there. She points the finger at Manning Clark who opened the can of orgy worms in his 1963 book *A Short History of Australia*. "Extra rations of rum were also issued," Clark wrote, "and soon there developed a drunken spree that ended only when the revellers were drenched by a violent rainstorm."

Clark's basis for this was the diary of our spruce beer brewer Arthur Bowes Smyth. According to Karskens, Clark realised he'd got it wrong after he re-read that diary. But by then, the myth of the wild orgy was out there and he couldn't put it back in the bottle. These days with the advent of the internet, the story about this bonkfest is all over the place.

If you read Smyth's entry for that night, the surgeon writes of how, by 6pm, the last of the female convicts had been taken by longboat to the shore. Here's what he wrote next, with some tinkering by myself to update the ye olde English.

"They were dressed in general very clean and some few amongst them might be said to be well dressed. The men convicts got to them very soon after they landed, and it is beyond my abilities to give a just description of the scene of debauchery and riot that ensued during the night.

"They had not been landed more than an hour before they had all got their tents pitched or anything in order to receive them, but there came on the most

violent storm of thunder, lightning and rain I ever saw. The lightning was incessant during the whole night and I never heard it rain faster.

"About 12 o'clock in the night one severe flash of lightning struck a very large tree in the centre of the camp under which some places were constructed to keep the sheep and hogs in: it split the tree from top to bottom; killed 5 sheep belonging to Major Ross and a pig of one of the Lieutenants. The severity of the lightning this and the two preceding nights leaves no room to doubt but many of the trees which appear burnt up to the tops of them were the effect of lightning."

Karskens suggests Smyth's account of a shoreline rootfest is dubious given he wasn't onshore at the time, he was still on the Lady Penrhyn anchored some distance off the coast. And it was dark and bucketing down. The good doctor would have to have had super eyesight to see exactly what was going on.

Were such an event of widespread rooting to have happened it would surely have appeared in journals, diaries and letters of the time. Yet famed diairist and British marine Watkin Tench never mentions it – he in fact writes that "nothing of a very atrocious nature" happened in February. Soldier and unrelenting misogynist Ralph Clark, who took a back seat to no one when it came to loathing the convict women, doesn't mention it in his diary either. Nor does a mention of it appear in any of the numerous letters written home. It seems no one but Smyth wrote a word of this happening – and even his details are very scant.

The remainder of the diary entry for the events of February 6 contains more detail, because it describes events happening much nearer to him. Namely, what the sailors on the Lady Penrhyn get up to after the female convicts leave.

"The sailors in our ship requested to have some grog to make merry with upon the women quitting the ship. Indeed the captain himself had no small reason to rejoice upon their being all safely landed and given into the care of the Governor, as he was under the penalty of £40 for every convict that was missing - for which reason he complied with the sailors' request and about the time they began to be elevated, the tempest came on.

"The scene which presented itself at this time and during the greater part of the night, beggars every description; some swearing, others quarrelling, others singing, not in the least regarding the tempest, though so violent."

It has been suggested that, when Manning Clark read this entry, he conflated the description of the shoreline action with what occurred on the ship. Indeed a quick reading can make it appear that what are actually tales of the sailors' antics *after* the women leave the ship could be construed as a description of the shoreline "orgy".

Something had to have happened on the shore that evening. It seems unlikely Bowes Smyth would have made the whole thing up. But no one else in the fleet seems to have mentioned it – and if you saw boatloads of men and women rooting around in the mud, I'd suggest that wouldn't be something easily forgotten. Also, I just don't buy the idea that the soldiers onshore would have let the convicts have at each other without intervening.

My two cents worth is that it seems quite likely there were some horizontal fraternisations that night. But the actual goings-on have since been substantially embellished to turn it into a massive sexual free-for-all. Now the orgy has become embedded in our national psyche, which is understandable because it *is* a good story. But I do wonder how much truth there is to it.

Before I end this chapter, I'd like to make one more aside. One about an alcohol-related event that doesn't involve rutting under the moonlight. But it does involve vegetables. For all the modern talk of the colony being awash with booze the law managed to take a surprising nine months before it found someone inebriated enough to be charged with public drunkenness. This poor fellow was convict Thomas Eccles, who appeared in court in October 1788 (the actual date, like Eccles' head at the time, is unclear). He faced two charges – being drunk and, while in that condition, stealing vegetables from the garden where he worked.

His curious defence was that the Captain of Marines was impressed with his work and gave him a tumbler of rum and, anyway, he only took radishes and left cauliflower. Not surprisingly, the court didn't buy it and found him guilty.

His punishment was to be dismissed from working in the garden – so as to be away from the vegetables' temptation – and be sent to the brickworks instead. There appears to be no word on whether he got drunk at his new job and tried to steal some bricks.

The Slab

THREE

AUSTRALIA'S FIRST HANGING

When you're going to start a nation with boatloads of lawbreakers it's surely not going to be long before some of them start breaking the law. Besides, it wasn't as if there was much else to do in the country at the time.

Therefore it was only going to be a matter of time before the authorities would have to dish out the severest of punishment – throwing a rope over the branch of a tall tree and looping the other end around some poor soul's neck. It took all of a month after the landing of the First Fleet for the noose to make its first appearance, and the poor soul was a man who well and truly had already more than used up all the luck he had in his short life.

He met his maker in a location where the colony's first jail would be built, at the bottom of a hill. Today, at the top of that hill, sits one of Sydney's best-known craft beer bars. But back in the early days of the colony, people would head to the top of that hill for a more macabre form of entertainment …

The Rocks in Sydney was one of the earliest places settled after the First Fleet arrived in Australia. Not because it was a little bit cool and funky and had water views but rather because it was close to where the fleet anchored. These days, at the top of one of The Rocks' steep streets sits Harts Pub – one of the city's best craft beer bars – in what was once a private residence on three levels.

It's actually fortunate the building is still there at all. In the early 20th century, when the bubonic plague broke out in The Rocks – by then a notorious slum (albeit one with water views) – the government reclaimed many buildings with the intent of knocking them down. Thousands of houses and buildings were inspected and hundreds destroyed, before the onset of World War I brought plans to a halt. Needless to say, the three-storey building that now houses Harts escaped the wrecking ball.

Admittedly, this tale of the first hanging in the colony is the one that has the most tenuous link to beer in the book. Today they drink beer at that pub on the hill – and get a feed, have a good time and maybe even enter the trivia contest. But it's what happened on that very same location back in the early days of the colony that interests us. Back then they gathered on the hill for a different reason – to watch people die. Down on George Street at the bottom of the hill was the settlement's first jail – and also the site of numerous hangings. At the top of the hill, people would crowd around to watch the hangman make people dance the "Paddington frisk", one of many slang terms for hanging.

Harts Pub's brewing arm Rocks Brewing Company has immortalised one of the 19th century executioners – Alexander Green – through its Hangman Pale Ale. But the site was used to dispatch convicts from a month after the First Fleet arrived. Today, a block down the hill from Harts Pub, on the corner of Essex and Harrington streets, is a green plaque marking the spot where a young fellow by the name of Thomas Barrett gained the unwanted historical footnote of being the first person hanged in Australia.

Barrett met his maker a scant few weeks after the arrival of the First Fleet. And it could be said his time was well and truly overdue; when he was hanged, it was the third time in six years he had been sentenced to death.

In 1782, Barrett was convicted of stealing a silver watch and other items and sentenced to death despite his defence of "I swear I didn't do it m'lud. Someone must have slipped them into my pockets. Yes, that's what happened" (which is pretty much the case: he and an accomplice were spotted running away from the scene of the crime. When he was caught soon after with the stolen property on his person, he said the other man was a total stranger who just handed the watch to him). Perhaps taking pity on him for mounting such a lame defence, the death sentence was later commuted to transportation to Nova Scotia on board a ship called the Mercury.

Not really all that keen on going to Canada, some of the convicts overtook the ship while still in British waters and made plans to head to Ireland. But bad weather forced them to return to Britain, where the law said "My God, how stupid are you?" and arrested Barrett and his mates, all of whom became known as "the Mercuries". He was also sentenced to hang for a second time, but again had the sentence commuted to transportation – this time to Australia.

He sailed on the First Fleet ship Charlotte, where he showed a special talent that did not result in being sentenced to death. An accomplished engraver, while on the ship under watch from the guards Barrett somehow managed to take pewter spoons, belt buckles and buttons and turn them into forged coins. He did such a good job that he managed to buy some supplies with them at Rio de Janeiro. The sellers only wised up later, when they dobbed Thomas in to the authorities. The First Fleet surgeon-general John White had a grudging admiration for Barrett's craftiness, writing in his diary that "the impression, milling, character in a word, the whole was so inimitably executed that had their metal been a little better, the fraud, I am convinced, would have passed undetected".

It was undoubtedly an impressive feat. He was in the hull of a small ship, in close quarters with other prisoners, where no fire to melt the pewter was available, while guards regularly stuck their heads in to make sure no one was doing anything wrong – like, say forging coins. Yet somehow he managed to work his magic. Though the fact a marine was caught trying to pass off Barrett's handiwork as real currency might suggest those who were meant to be guarding him turned a blind eye at the right time.

White liked Barrett's skills so much he commissioned what is likely to be white Australia's first piece of art. In the days between arriving at Botany Bay and then buggering off to Sydney Cove, the surgeon-general commissioned Barrett to make a commemorative medallion to mark the fleet's arrival. Featuring the Charlotte on one side and a rather dry itinerary of the voyage from Britain on the other, it's become known as the Charlotte medal.

However much goodwill Barrett's fancy medallion garnered for him, it only lasted a month. On February 27, he and three other convicts, Henry Lavell, Joseph Hall and John Ryan, were caught with food stolen from the government store. History is silent on whether Barrett tried the "some stranger gave it to me" defence again. If he did try that one again, it was just as successful as the other time.

The court tried and convicted all four of them and sentenced all but Ryan to hang. Ryan, adjudged to be a receiver rather than a stealer, got 300 lashes instead. Which was better than being killed, but still would have hurt quite a bit.

At around 5pm on February 27, the three condemned men walked to the tree at the base of the hill where they would hang. All the convicts were rounded up and made to watch, perhaps in the hope it might discourage a few from breaking the law. Or maybe it was because there was no TV and everyone was bored. At the last minute a sentry rushed up the hill with a stay of execution for Lavell and Hall. "haha, not for you Barrett. Sucked in," the sentry may have said. And so the man who had twice dodged a death sentence found his luck had well and truly run out.

"Abt. 1/2 after 6 o'clock pm he express[ed] not the least signs of fear," wrote one witness, surgeon Arthur Bowes Smyth (who, unlike in the last chapter, actually *was* at the scene this time), "till he mounted the ladder then he turn'd very pale & seem'd very much shock'd."

Maybe the shock was because he realised no one would intervene to save him yet again. There was a bit of time for that to happen; the hangman was not at all keen on stringing up Barrett so he dawdled with the rope for ages. So long in fact that a soldier had to tell him "quit pissfarting around or I'll shoot you". Or words to that effect.

In the end, there was no saviour for Barrett; he was hanged at about 6.30pm. As one would expect given Barrett was dangling from a rope roughly slung over a tree branch, he didn't go easy; he kicked and struggled as he slowly asphyxiated. His body dangled there for about an hour before being cut down and buried near the gallows tree.

If you're heading to Harts Pub sometime, maybe you could stop on the corner of Harrington and Essex streets and spare a thought or two for Thomas Barrett, the man who managed to cheat death twice but found that the third time really wasn't the charm.

FOUR
BATTLE OF OUR FIRST BREWERS

For quite a while there was a company with a brand named after a man. And it liked to claim that this man was the first person in Australia to ever brew a beer. And everyone figured that was just fine.

Then another company came along with another brand named after a different man. And this company also liked to claim it was this man who made the first beer in our country. But no one really cared because so few people even knew the beer that bore this man's name even existed.

That changed when a very big company bought the brand named after the second man and put the beers in all their many stores right across the country. They even made their beers look eerily similar to that brand named after the first man. And some people started to wonder what was the truth, because one thing was certain – these men couldn't both be our first brewer.

So one of them just had to be telling porkies …

There are two breweries using the title of "Australia's first brewer" – James Squire and John Boston - and simple logic tells you they can't both be right.

But in a way, they're both wrong, because neither of these breweries actually has anything to do with these real once-living and breathing figures of history and their achievements (whether they actually were the first or not). The brewery bearing James' name emerged in 1998 after an enterprise started by Chuck Hahn was rebranded as the craft beer arm of mega-brewery Lion and took the name of James Squire for their beers. The brewery itself was renamed the Malt Shovel Brewery – after the real Squire's brewery-tavern The Malting Shovel.

So we have a brewery and a range of beers named for James Squire created more than 150 years after the real person named James Squire died. Hell, the Malt Shovel Brewery isn't even in the same spot as Squire's original. There's no connection at all other than the name.

It's the same deal with John Boston, a beer brand started by the Wine Society in 2009 that went pretty much nowhere until they sold it to Woolworths in 2013. The supermarket giant then went about revamping the packaging so it looked uncannily like that of the other "first brewer" James Squire and seeing that it got very good positioning in all the bottle shops it owned – and that included small chains like Dan Murphy's and BWS.

Both beers have also appropriated the lives of these men, so on their packaging you'll get little snippets of their shenanigans and the beers are named for certain events that are linked to them. For instance, the James Squire beer The Constable refers to the time later in his life that he served as a district constable. And a John

Boston beer is called The Surprize, named after the ship he and his family boarded to sail to Australia. Though they inaccurately spell it as "Surprise"

It's a whole lot of detail of the lives of two men to which neither brewery has any direct connection. Though, of course, they'd never tell you that because they'd like you to think there is. Like there's been a descendant of James Squire's working for Lion for the last 150-odd years. Oh puleeeze.

Anyway, when we talk about the real people, which one of them *is* Australia's the first brewer? Let's assume it was between the two of them and there wasn't some other person lost to history who beat both of them to the punch. See, there is a lack of accurate, impartial records to conclusively say who was first. Which is fair enough; it's not as if some diarist in the late 18th century would have said, "I must write down the details about our first brewer in case, sometime in the future, two big corporations get into a passive-aggressive fight about who it was".

The year of John Boston's first brew was 1796 and there is some contemporary evidence to support it. The NSW colony's judge advocate David Collins makes mention of Boston's beer in his work *An Account of the English Colony in New South Wales*, published in 1798.

Collins wrote that it was made at Sydney and "brewed from Indian corn, properly malted, and bittered with the leaves and stalks of the love-apple, (Lycopersicum, a species of Solarium) or, as it was more commonly called in the settlement, the Cape gooseberry. Mr Boston found this succeeded so well, that he erected at some expense a building proper for the business, and was, when the ships sailed, engaged in brewing beer from the abovementioned materials, and in making soap."

So that's a reference made in 1798 just two years after Boston was meant to have brewed it. Incidentally, the "love apple"? Well, that's basically a tomato – Collins got it wrong.

When it comes to James Squire, he isn't mentioned in Collins' account at all (nor does he appear in Robert Hughes legendary and voluminous book *The Fatal Shore* - but Boston does). With Squire, it seems the only evidence he was brewing before Boston is his own recollections 30 years later. In 1819 Squire appeared before the Bigge Inquiry, which was set up to examine the performance of the colonial government. Squire told the inquiry,

"I have been in the colony from its earliest establishment and for 30 years I have been a brewer. At first I lived in Sydney, and brewed beer in small quantities. I sold it then for 4d per quart and made it from some hops that I got from the Daedalus. I also brewed for General Grose and Col Patterson for their own consumption from English malt. I have been established at Kissing Point as a brewer for 28 years, and have brewed beer from Indian corn and colonial barley."

According to Squire's evidence, he had been brewing in 1789. And there is independent confirmation of this, in the form of a ship's list from the HMS Daedalus, a supply ship that arrived in Sydney in 1793. It brought in 16 cases of essence of malt, seven casks of malt and four casks of hops. If Squire hadn't used those ingredients to brew beer it would seem pretty strange that he knew the ship had some on board and would still remember it 30 years later. That means he was brewing in 1793, if not before, which certainly puts him ahead of Boston. Also, for what it's worth, Squire came on the First Fleet in 1788 – on the Charlotte, the same ship as Thomas Barrett of the previous chapter.

Squire's being in the First Fleet means he had a head-start on Boston, who arrived six years later in 1794 and isn't recorded as making his first beer until two years after that. It's hard to imagine Squire didn't do anything beer-wise for those eight years. For this reason my money's on Squire as being the first brewer, which means the claims made by those in the Boston camp are a bit bogus.

Leaving aside the fight about who actually was first to get a beer going, the stories of Squire and Boston are quite interesting. Boston didn't like reactionary Britain and so decided to pack up and go to Australia. In December 1793 he wrote to the British authorities to promote how awesome he was and how the colony simply could not do without him.

"I was brought up a surgeon and apothecary, but have never since followed that profession. I have since made my particular study those parts of chemistry that are more particularly usefull [sic] in trade and business. I have, therefore, a knowledge of brewing, distilling, sugar-making, vinegar-making, soap-making, etc. I have been in business as distiller, but was unsuccessful. I likewise have a theoretical and some practical knowledge of agriculture."

In other words, he knows a little bit about a lot of things but perhaps not enough to be proficient in any of them. At any rate, he made it to Australia as part of the Second Fleet, sailing on The Surprize. Not long after arriving, he convinced the higher-ups he could extract the salt from seawater (salt was very much in need for preserving food). So they set him up with some choice real estate at what would become Bennelong Point (home of the Sydney Opera House) and seven convicts to help with his work. But it soon transpired that his mouth was writing cheques his butt couldn't cash. As a salt extractor he was crap – he produced less than four bushels of the stuff in over a month.

By 1796 he'd turned his hand to brewing beer, with the help of an encyclopaedia – because the internet hadn't been invented yet. He built a windmill on Bennelong Point to help grind the corn that he used in the beer. He was also making soap at the same time, which suggests the market for his beer wasn't that great. That may have been because, as it was made with the leaves and stalks of the tomato plant, it probably wasn't the tastiest beer known to mankind.

In 1801 he and his family packed up and left the colony on a ship he'd bought called the El Plumier and stayed away for several years - partially because it seems some Spaniards stole his ship. He eventually got hold of another ship and headed back to Australia in May, 1804. Five months later, he left again. Passing Tonga he was sucked in by the apparently friendly natives and landed there. Where he was killed and eaten, so the story goes. Though how we know that is anyone's guess; it's not like the natives could tell anyone "John Boston? Yeah, we ate that guy. Tasted a bit like tomatoes".

There is a lot more information around on James Squire (which might have prompted the modern-day brewery to swipe his name). There's a chance he could have become America's first brewer and not Australia's - in 1774 he ransacked a house in England and ran into two constables as he escaped. He was sentenced to seven years transportation to the United States but got out of it after electing to serve in the army for two years.

He gave crime another go in 1784 - or at least this was the next time he got caught - when he stole five hens and four roosters from his neighbour's yard. This time he didn't escape transportation and the chicken thief was sentenced to seven years in Australia, sailing there on the First Fleet ship The Charlotte.

The fleet arrived in 1788 and, a year later he got caught stealing a pound of pepper and some herbs from the hospital stores where he worked. He claimed at the time the herb was for his pregnant wife. He was sentenced to 300 lashes - 150 now and the rest to be handed out at a later date. This is where the One Fifty Lashes beer gets its name.

After he became a free man, in 1795 he was granted a plot of land at Kissing Point, in what is now the Sydney suburb of Ryde. The official story given by the company that now bears his name is Kissing Point was so named because boats would "kiss" the shore as they passed. There is a different story that suggests this was the place where prostitutes plied their trade and "Kissing Point" was a polite euphemism for what actually happened there.

Squire later acquired the land next to his plot at Kissing Point and, after the other freed men didn't claim the nearby plots they had been granted, he snapped those up too - building up a huge estate of more than 400 hectares. He eventually grew the first Australian hops (probably Pride of Ringwood - beer geek joke!) in 1805 and set up the Malting Shovel brewery and pub a year later.

Then he got busy, becoming a farmer, a baker and a district constable, as well as acting as a bit of a philanthropists to his poorer neighbours. He died on May 16, 1822, and was mourned in what some stated was the biggest funeral in the colony.

His tombstone read, "He arrived in the colony in the First Fleet, and by integrity and industry acquired and maintained an unsullied reputation. Under his care the hop plant was first cultivated in this settlement and the first brewery was erected, which progressively matured to perfection. As a father, a husband, a friend and a Christian, he lived respected and died lamented."

His brewery didn't last much longer. Squire's son, unimaginatively named James, took over the brewery until he died in 1826. Two years later his son-in-law Thomas Farnell reopened it until poor health forced its closure in 1834, this time for good.

Incidentally, his grandson, James Squire Farnell became the first Australian-born Premier of NSW in 1877. He served for just a year.

One more interesting footnote about James Squire is that both his parents' families were embroiled in one of the more well-known criminal mysteries of the 1700s. His parents were Timothy Squires (or Squire) and Mary Wells. In 1754, the year of his birth, relatives of both of his parents were caught up in what became known as The Canning Affair.

It revolved around the disappearance of English servant Elizabeth Canning on New Year's Day 1753. She turned up about a month later on January 29, her face and hands black with dirt, dressed in a petticoat and with a dirty rag tied around her head and soaked with blood. She delivered an incredible tale – two men had attacked her, robbing her, stripping her of her clothes and then knocking her unconscious. Then she woke and the two men forced her to walk to a house, where a woman said she would be turned into a prostitute. She refused and was placed in an upstairs room, where she remained until being able to escape by pulling some boards away from a window and walking five miles home.

Supporters of Canning soon identified the house as that owned by Susannah Wells – an older relative of James Squire's mother.

Warrant officers brought her to the house to see if she could identify her captors – she could, pointing the finger at Wells, an old woman there by the name of Mary Squires (James' great grandmother) and several other family members.

The media, drawn to the story of an 18-year-old girl being kidnapped and threatened with prostitution, reported all the details of the trials. Canning attended the trials, followed by a large crowd of her supporters. Both Wells and Squires were found guilty; the former was branded on her hand and jailed for six months, the latter was sentenced to be hanged.

And there the matter would have ended, but for the curiosity of another judge, Sir Crisp Gascoyne. He didn't believe Canning's story at all. After interviewing a number of witnesses, he concluded the Squires were not in the area at the time of Canning's kidnapping and therefore couldn't have been involved. He ordered Canning arrested for perjury and the papers again went wild. Gascoyne wrote to King George II, who first granted a stay of execution for Mary Squires before eventually pardoning her altogether.

Wells wasn't so lucky, having already served her sentence. And had her hand branded. And Canning? She was found guilty of perjury and sentenced to seven years' transportation to America. She married there, had four children and died in 1773.

To this day, mystery surrounds what actually happened to Canning. Was she an innocent kidnapped by thugs? Or did she invent the whole story in an effort to cover up a month spent as a willing prostitute? Both theories have been put forward to explain those events in January 1753. Another theory – which is the most intriguing is that she was kidnapped by a man who wanted to keep her in the house as his mistress. Stricken with fear – and likely raped – Canning goes into a fugue state where she remembers nothing of what happens. The rapist tires of her and hands her over to Wells, who can't get rid of her. Until Canning "wakes up", finds she's in captivity and makes her escape.

Once home she makes up a story that fits what she thinks must have happened and then comes to believe it. Which means she did commit perjury, but unwittingly, as she couldn't recall what really happened.

FIVE
BENNELONG AND JAMES SQUIRE

It would not be stretching the truth at all to say a lot of the early settlers in Sydney disliked the Aboriginal population. At best they were a curiosity – whenever one was captured and brought to town the locals would flock to gawp and gaze.

But usually, the Aboriginal population was met with gunfire. Or smallpox. Because, really, they were in the way of white people taking the land and setting up their society. If the Aboriginal people were serious about things, they would have already built houses and stuff. Maybe even invented a wheel or two.

Not all the settlers were this way. Governor Arthur Phillip encouraged people to show restraint (ie don't murder them) But he still authorised several kidnappings, which are really never cool.

Another appears to have been James Squire. the real James Squire, that is, not the brewery that bears his name. He befriended Bennelong – perhaps the most well-known Aboriginal man of his time. It's not known exactly how they became mates, but Squire did care enough to bury Bennelong on his farm at Kissing Point when he died…

As we've seen in the previous chapter, the people at Lion aren't at all shy about appropriating the history of convict brewer James Squire. One Fifty Lashes gets its name from the punishment Squire got from stealing beer ingredients from the NSW colony stores while The Constable was inspired by the man's later incarnation as a police officer.

Even the shadier side of Squire's life gets used for beer names; his way with the ladies – he had one wife and three mistresses is immortalised in Four 'Wives' pilsener (kudos, however, to the brewery for adding inverted commas around 'Wives', as he never married at least two of them. Punctuation, especially the location of apostrophes, seems to confuse our mainstream brewers). His work in conning freed convicts out of their land grants - a total of 392 hectares - is where The Swindler gets its name.

With so much of Squire's life rife for corporate plundering, it's quite odd that there isn't a beer that celebrates the surprising friendship between Squire and Bennelong, perhaps the most well-known Aboriginal of the time of white settlement. Bennelong even died on Squire's property and was buried there in 1813.

Bennelong is a fascinating figure in Australian colonial history. He lived among the English settlers for a time before visiting England for three years and finally returned home to his own people.

When he headed to Australia with the First Fleet, governor Arthur Phillip was under instructions from King George III (yes, the mad one) to "endeavour, by every possible means, to open an intercourse with the natives, and to conciliate their affections, enjoining all subjects to live in amity and kindness". Phillip apparently read that as "kidnap one or two of them". And so, one November day at Manly Cove, Bennelong and another Aboriginal man called Colbee were captured and taken to Sydney Cove.

Not at all surprisingly, Colbee wasn't chuffed with being nabbed by these strange white creatures and dragged to their place, and so he promptly escaped. This truly seemed to make a few of those strange white creatures somewhat indignant; "How rude of the blighter to run away after all that effort we put in to kidnapping him," they might have said. A little surprisingly, Bennelong hung around; though a description by marine and diarist Watkin Tench suggests he wasn't entirely cool with what whitey had done. Tench described the captured Bennelong as being "of good statue (sic) and stoutly made, with a bold intrepid countenance, which bespoke defiance and revenge". Kidnap me and my countenance would bespoke things like that too.

Bennelong lived in Government House, picked up some English customs - like wearing clothes and thinking about kidnapping people (maybe) - and taught the white folk a thing or two about his way of life. He also picked up the white man's fondness for alcohol. While other Aboriginal people had turned their noses up at a glass of wine or rum when it was offered by white settlers Bennelong took to it almost immediately. He grew so used to wine that he initially thought it was called "the King", because he noticed while sitting at the Governor's table, the white guests would raise their glasses and offer a toast to "the King". Even after Bennelong knew the actual name was "wine" he would still refer to the beverage as "King".

Then, in May 1790 six months after his kidnapping, Bennelong thought "I'm done with this", jumped the fence at Government House and walked away. Cue the indignant English white guys again.

He dodged The Man for three months, until he was found at Manly Cove; Phillip turned up for the reunion but an Aboriginal man with Bennelong gave the white folk something to really be indignant about by spearing Phillip through the shoulder. Contrary to the behaviour of many other white settlers when confronted with angry black men, Phillip did not order death to all Aboriginal people in a 10-mile radius. Instead, he was convinced it was a misunderstanding and told the soldiers accompanying him not to shoot them dead. Though he did draw a pistol from under his coat and fire a shot as the Englishmen rushed back to the ship.

Most historians have suggested his comrade's behaviour shocked Bennelong, but Keith Vincent Smith has written that Bennelong orchestrated the whole thing as a way of evening the score for his kidnapping. Which makes sense; someone kidnaps you it's really hard to let bygones be bygones. So, with the historical slate wiped clean, they could start afresh. Also, eyewitness reports mention Bennelong laying the spear at the feet of the man who would soon throw it into Phillip's shoulder.

There have been claims made that the spearing incident was the first time Bennelong and James Squire crossed paths. The claim goes that he was there at Manly Cove as a member of Phillip's guard that day. Much of the claiming seems to come from the James Squire brewery media guff, so make of that what you will. Captain David Collins, Lieutenant Henry Waterhouse and Arthur Phillip were on the beach that day. They all left accounts of that day and none of them mention James Squire's name. Similarly, there are numerous second-hand accounts – including one from marine and diarist Watkin Tench – and they don't mention him either.

They do mention a ship's crew waiting back on the shore with the boat, so it's not outside the realms of possibility that Squire was in that crew. But if he was one of Phillip's most-trusted guards – as the story claims – wouldn't he have been by the governor's side when he was confronting the natives and not 40 or 50 metres away? You ask me, I call shenanigans on the suggestion that Squire was there.

Anyway, having felt that the spearing made everything even-stevens, Bennelong returned to the colony, helping to foster improved relations and a decline in spearing incidents between the two groups. He and Phillip got along like a house on fire; speaking of houses, Phillip even had one built for him - on the site where the Sydney Opera House now stands.

After about two years – in December 1792 – Phillip decided to return to England. Bennelong's frown was turned upside down when he was told he could come along. So he and another Aboriginal man named Yemmerawanne travelled to England, along with a few other colonial curiosities intended to amuse the Brits back home – four kangaroos and a handful of dingoes.

Days after their arrival, *Lloyd's Evening Post* wrote "From the description given of the natives of Jackson's Bay they appear to be a race totally incapable of civilisation..." According to academic Kate Fullagher's essay on Bennelong's time in Britain, this entry was the sole time Bennelong's visit was mentioned in a British newspaper. That suggests visits from natives of lands conquered by the might of the British Empire were old hat by this time. Or maybe it was just that Bennelong, with his penchant for wearing ruffled lacy shirts and fancy waistcoats and a familiarity with English custom, didn't come across as the stereotypical savage native. Perhaps he should have speared a few of them.

Bennelong returned to Sydney without Phillip in September 1795, but preferred to forsake the colonists. "Upon his return to the Colony," wrote George Howe in the 1818 *New South Wales Pocket Almanac*, "he fell off spontaneously into his early habits, and in spite of everything that could be done to him in the order of civilisation, he took to the bush, and only occasionally visited Government House."

Despite the commonly held view that Bennelong was a man stranded between two cultures and accepted in neither, he does seem to have successfully returned to the tribal lifestyle at this point, leading a 100-strong clan along the Parramatta River, between Kissing Point and Parramatta.

It was in this same area that James Squire set up his farm with the 12-hectare land grant he got after serving his sentence. He managed to parlay that into a massive property after buying up other land grants for a one pathetic shilling each, amassing an extra 392ha of land. What a con artist.

It's around this time that the two men met. While the circumstances are not known, historians reckon Bennelong regularly wandered onto Squire's land and, after neither speared the other, they eventually became friends. Indeed they became such good friends Bennelong was invited to live on Squire's land, apparently finding it better than the waterfront cottage Phillip had given him.

Bennelong died on Squire's land on January 2, 1813. Some claim he drowned in a vat of Squire's beer, which does seem to fit the "drunken Aboriginal" cliche a little too perfectly. That said,

Bennelong did have a problem with alcohol; it seems more likely he died of an illness exacerbated by booze and the wounds suffered from relentless payback battles.

On his friend's death, Squire insisted on erecting a plaque over Bennelong's grave. And then the *Sydney Gazette* chose to piss all over that grave – metaphorically speaking – in a staggeringly brutal obituary.

"Bennelong died on Sunday morning last at Kissing Point. Of this veteran champion of the native tribe little favourable can be said. His voyage to and benevolent treatment in Great Britain produced no change whatever in his manners and inclinations, which were naturally barbarous and ferocious.

"The principal officers of Government had for many years endeavoured, by the kindest of usage, to wean him from his original habits and draw him into a relish for civilised life; but every effort was in vain exerted and for the last few years he has been but little noticed. His propensity for drunkenness was inordinate; and when in that state he was insolent, menacing and overbearing.

"In fact, he was a thorough savage, not to be warped from the form and character that nature gave him by all the efforts that mankind could use."

Given the fact the colony was largely made up of criminals, that drunkenness among the whites was not at all unusual and Bennelong was expected to be grateful for being kidnapped, these claims seem supremely hypocritical.

The location of Bennelong's grave was a mystery for around 200 years. In 1988 there was a bicentennial plaque placed in Cleves Park in the Sydney suburb of Putney, which read as follows:

"Bennelong was an Aborigine who befriended the first colonists, lived for a while as Governor Phillip's guest and visited England where he became the

toast of society. Following his death, he was buried hereabouts beside his wife and Nanbaree, another Aborigine."

The use of the word "hereabouts" seems far too cavalier, if you ask me. Like they lost something and can't be buggered looking very hard for it.

Then, in 2011, someone did start looking - and he found it. Environmental scientist Peter Mitchell managed to pinpoint it to the front yard of a home in Putney. But, working with Ryde council, the location was kept a secret at the time. Apparently not even the home owners were told at the time who was buried under their lawn.

Dr Mitchell told journalist Eamon Duff in 2011 that it was "vital" that the exact location remained secret because "the whole question of what to do next is likely to be controversial in the broader community … It's not a question Ryde Council, or I, can resolve. This is now a significant matter for the Aboriginal community. Consultation is essential. They must decide what they want."

Since then, the location has been given as the corner of Watson St and Hordern Ave, Putney. But it appears little has been done, much to the ire of Metropolitan Local Aboriginal Land Council's Allen Madden, who said "If it is him we want him out from under the footpath".

But the final decision was made to leave the grave untouched because it was too fragile to disturb. "It has been resolved that nothing else will now happen on that corner," Dr Mitchell said.

"We will leave it as it is and it will become a registered Aboriginal site so if there's any future possibility of disturbance on the site, that will flag it."

Incidentally, the exact location of Squire's grave seems a bit of a mystery too. He was buried in Sydney's Devonshire Street Cemetery, which is now the site of Central Station. When the station was being constructed, his body was exhumed and moved to a cemetery at Botany where he apparently was laid to rest under a tombstone too faded to read.

The Slab

SIX
GOVERNMENT BECOMES A BREWER

These days the government seems keen to get us to drink less beer. They issue drinking guidelines that include how many beers you can have each day without slowly killing yourself – or something like that. Some people object to these guidelines as being absurdly low, which I translate as "hey, I drink more than that. You're making me feel bad about it. So rather than slow down my drinking, I'm going to mock your advice".

The government decides all the bars and clubs in Kings Cross need to have lockouts at 1.30am and can't serve booze after 3am. Why? Because a few numbskulls figure it's a top idea to get drunk and then punch unsuspecting people in the head. Some people say it's not alcohol that's making them punch on but some inherent character flaw. I'd suggest they have a point, but I'd also wonder why someone needs to be able to get a drink at 3am. Then again, I'm old and a big night for me is still being awake at 10pm.

The government also decides bottle shops have to close at 10pm. Some people figure they should be able to buy beer whenever they want. Me, I figure you just need to plan things a bit better so you don't run out of beer after 10pm.

Well, once upon a time, the government wanted us to drink MORE beer, not less. They were so keen on the idea, they actually started up their own brewery. It didn't go so well ...

These days it's hard to imagine a government encouraging people to drink beer, let alone set up its own brewery. But that's just what happened in 1803 when the Parramatta Brewery was built with government money at the behest of NSW Governor Philip King.

There was a sound reason behind King's brewery plans - and that was the fact that beer gets you less pissed than the same serving of rum. And it seems the early NSW settlers were getting into the rum and other spirits a bit too often.

This was the time leading into the Rum Rebellion - where the NSW Corps marched on Government House, arrested Governor William Bligh and the colony fell under military rule. That would take place five years later – and didn't really have that much to do with rum anyway. Australia's first military coup was more about a power struggle between the military and civilian elites.

Hell, it wasn't even known as the Rum Rebellion at the time – that name came about 50 years later. But Australians always seems to love a story about itself that involves alcohol, and so the tag "Rum Rebellion" stuck.

This isn't to say rum or whatever other spirits weren't being drunk – they were. Spirits served as a form of currency for a time, especially when it came to getting convicts to work for you. However, some modern historians suggest the idea of early Sydney being awash with booze was a byproduct of demographics. Between the convicts and the soldiers, the population in the early years of the colony was very much male. Without the sobering influences of women, children, employment and community, the men tended to drink a lot more. Some studies contend that, once allowances are made for the large male population, the per capita level of drinking in early Australia was really nothing special at all.

This – and the NSW Corps monopolising of the spirit market – was enough an issue for Governor King to think the government brewing beer and ensuring it was sold at a subsided price were both very good ideas. Others liked the idea too, including British MP Lord Hobart, who wrote to Governor King in 1802:

"The introduction of beer into general use among the inhabitants would certainly lessen the consumption of spirituous liquors. I have therefore in conformity with your suggestion taken measures for furnishing the colony with a supply of ten tons of porter, six bags of hops, and two complete sets of brewing materials."

There may well have been another factor motivating the men to make this decision. Both men would have been old enough to have knowledge of the gin craze that plagued London from 1700 to about 1760. That was a time when it seemed most of London's poor were walking around stonkered - as artist William Hogarth's legendary work *Gin Lane* vividly illustrates. That's the one with a woman in the centre frame sitting on stairs so blind on gin that she doesn't realise she's dropped her baby over the railing. Behind her is pictured a London of vice and degradation.

The gin craze happened because the country was at war with France and had placed a ban on imported spirits. To fill the gap, they offered tax breaks for people to distill spirits from English corn. Which an awful lot of people did. By 1721, English Excise and Revenue records stated around 25 per cent of London's residents were making tax-free booze – an astonishing 9.1 million litres of it a year – and sold at any one of a staggering 5000 gin shops (one of which carried the sign "Drunk for a penny, dead drunk for two pence, clean straw for nothing." The straw was for sleeping on, by the way). Now there is no way things will end well with that much cheap booze floating around.

Now, what happens to the price of something when you have a glut? Yep, it goes down. So the poor people could literally get drunk for just pennies. Many of them did, as an escape from the misery of being poor. And they did it over and over again.

Not unexpectedly, gin was soon blamed as "the principal cause of all the vice & debauchery committed among the inferior sort of people". And it led to people doing some horrendous things to get cash for more booze; in 1734 Judith Dufour confessed to murdering her own two-year-old daughter, so she could sell the child's clothes for money to buy 60ml of gin.

Parliament had to pass no fewer than five Gin Acts (1729, 1736, 1743, 1747 and 1751) before the gin tide was staunched – which suggests either an inept government or a population who really, really liked their gin and wouldn't give it up easily. So it's no wonder Governor King wanted to try and nip the colony's developing dependence on any sort of spirit in the bud. In beer, he chose the same alternative as *Gin Lane* artist Hogarth. The artist also created a lesser-known companion piece, *Beer Street*, that shows a more civil and humane society. "[Beer Street] was given as a contrast," Hogarth explained, "where the invigorating liquor is recommended in order [to] drive the other out of vogue. Here all is joyous and thriving [.] Industry and jollity go hand in hand."

After having the bags of hops, brewing utensils and other items sent out by Lord Hobart, Governor King got to work building the new brewery in 1803. Well, technically, he got to work ordering the convicts to build it, on the corner of George and O'Donnell streets in Parramatta. In 1804, it was finished and in September brewer Thomas Rushton had the first batches out. By the end of the year, more than 19,000 litres had been produced. The beer was sold to licenced people and the government would set the maximum price they could charge the punters.

But the brewery was quite a failure - according to Keith M Deutsher's detailed book *The Breweries of Australia*, it wasn't hard to see why. Deutsher says each employee at the brewery got an astonishing 20 litres of beer a week – the equivalent of nearly three cases. And there were quite a few employees; with perks like that it's not hard to understand why everyone wanted to work there. Despite getting three cases a week, there was still widespread theft among the employees and so, at the end of 1805, Governor King shut down the brewery.

In February 1806 the brewer Rushton took out a lease on the brewery, with payment made in beer. He didn't renew the lease in 1808, preferring to start his own brewery at the Brickfields, near what is now Darling Harbour. The property was offered for rent in 1809 and again in 1810 but there were no takers.

And so the government never got into the business of making beer again. Since then they've found it far easier to tax what others make.

The Slab

Easter Egg #1

You know how films have "Easter eggs" - a little secret bit hidden somewhere for the dedicated to find? Well, I'm doing something similar with this book. In several places throughout *The Slab* there are little bonus stories like this one. Those who dip in and read a chapter here and there will likely miss them, but it's a bit of a reward for those reading cover to cover. And who doesn't like rewards?

Okay, now let me tell you how beer may have led to a false start by the First Fleet. So we're back in 1787, May 12 to be precise and the First Fleet is anchored at Portsmouth, England. That evening, Captain Arthur Phillip decides to head off and gives the signal to the 11 ships in the fleet to pull up their anchors. Some of the ships start moving but, when Phillip looks back, he sees "several of the convoy not getting under way, through some irregularity in the seamen", according to the fleet's chief surgeon John White.

Phillip sends Lieutenant King over to the ships to see what the hell they're doing. According to White, King "soon adjusted the difficulties that had arisen, as they were found to proceed more from intoxication than from any nautical causes". So they were too hungover to sail.

Because some people have to wreck a good story, King himself says it was a sort of mini-mutiny. He would later say the seamen hadn't been paid for nearly seven months and wanted some cash to buy things for the trip, while their masters were keen to withhold the money until they set sail so the seamen would be forced to buy the same goods on board - albeit at a substantial mark-up.

So which is true? Well, either of them could be. The mutiny sounds quite plausible; with the masters keen to wring a few extra bucks out of the sailors. But the idea the sailors might tie one on the night before leaving on an eight-month sea voyage makes sense too.

On the morning of May 13, 1787, Phillip tried to set sail again and this time the seamen on those other ships – whether because they were sober or had been able to do some last-minute shopping – followed him out into the open ocean.

SEVEN
COOPERS – THE ORIGINAL CRAFT BREWER

Kids today, they don't know how lucky they've got it. These days, craft beer grows on trees. You can find it almost everywhere. Hell, even supermarket bottle shops stock craft beer. But it wasn't always the case – for an eternity, if you wanted something different to the lagers put out by the mainstream breweries you had one choice. Well, unless you were a homebrewer and could make whatever you wanted, but let's assume you weren't.

So you only had the one choice for something with a bit of ooomph, a bit of flavour. And that one thing was a bottle of Coopers, which sported a different colour depending on what sort of beer it was – red for the sparkling ale, yellow for the stout and green for the pale ale. Red, yellow, green - kind of like a Coopers traffic light.

Those kids of today are so spoilt, some of them don't even consider Coopers to be "craft". Which is insane – the man and the brewery were craft before the word "craft" was a thing.

Have some respect for the history of beer, kids …

If Thomas Cooper's wife Ann had a stronger constitution it's possible the oldest family-owned brewery in Australia may never have existed. And, if Thomas had stuck it out at his first job, we'd be buying Coopers shoes and not beers.

Thomas, a pregnant Ann and their two children left England and arrived in Adelaide in 1852. After he got here, Thomas was a bit hit and miss when it came to landing a job. He started out in his trade as a shoemaker before deciding to chuck that in and become a mason. He learned that trade well enough that he was able to build his own house.

But the man with a short attention span got jack of building houses and so, by 1857, he'd changed his mind again and became a dairy farmer. Five years later, in 1862, came the moment that would change not only his career, but the lives of many other people would come to populate the Cooper family tree. One day in 1862, Ann wasn't feeling too perky (perhaps it was stress brought on by her husband's inability to get a steady job), so Thomas brewed some beer from a recipe of her's – she was an innkeeper's daughter. Why Thomas felt beer would be just the tonic for a sick person seems a bit strange but for a long time there was a belief that beer was good for you. Yeah, the same thing that can give you hangovers and take you for a ride on the porcelain bus. They thought *that* was a health food. Weirdos.

Presumably, Ann got better – Thomas' beer certainly didn't kill her (which was a risk with the dubious brewing practices and dodgy ingredients used by some brewers at the time – as we shall see in a page or two). It must have been a decent drop because some of his neighbours heard about it and wanted to buy some, which made Thomas decide to swap careers again and become a brewer.

The official story has Thomas' first recorded batch as brewed on May 13, 1862, but logic would suggest that was not the beer made for Ann. At the time he was brewing for his wife, it would have been seen as a one-off and so he would have been unlikely to keep a record of it. Keeping a record of a beer suggests a man planning to make brewing a regular occurrence, which Thomas only decided to do later.

That first batch has gone down in company lore as a pale ale designated "A", made with four bushels of English malt and eight pounds of Kent hops in 46 gallons of water. To cover a few markets he split that first brew into a straight pale ale and a somewhat heavier ale – selling both on a per dozen basis. And like any homebrewer, Thomas reused old bottles – beer, whisky and any other type he could get his hands on. It was a necessity as there was no glassworks in the South Australian colony.

In his first year as a brewer, he made a brew about once every two weeks. That was probably all he had time for because, as well as all the other brewery tasks like sourcing ingredients, finding and cleaning bottles, selling and delivering beer, Thomas had also kept his dairy farm and milk run going so as to have a second source of income. It seemed he finally got the message that having a paying job is always a good idea.

By the end of his first year, Ann had gotten sick of him brewing around the house and so he borrowed money to build a proper brewhouse with better equipment. And Ann got her house back. Thomas even sold his milk run, which was an indication of how confident he felt in making money out of making beer. Or maybe he was just sick of getting up really early to deliver milk.

Thomas also took the process of brewing seriously, which may account for his success. In a letter to his brother, he pointed out he wasn't a cowboy like some of the other brewers around the place.

"There are some half dozen breweries besides ours in and about Adelaide but they all use a good deal of sugar and so on for brewing, but we use only malt and hops consequently, ours being pure the doctors recommend it to all their patients."

Sugar was used by brewers as a cheap substitute for malt, while still creating beer with a similar alcohol level. But it tends to taste disgusting. So by using better ingredients, Thomas was bound to get a better-tasting beer. As for the idea of doctors recommending beer to their patients, well, that's likely to be the "lesser of two evils" approach. If a patient is going to pour beer down their throat, they could at least drink one that's not going to make you sick. And some of them did make you sick – even after a single glass.

Many beers that were brewed at this time had what was called the "colonial twang" (in an ad for his beers Thomas more delicately spoke of "the peculiar flavour of colonial ales" of his rivals). That twang is an unpleasant taste brought about by beer being fermented at higher than ideal temperatures – the climate in Australia was much warmer than brewers were used to in England and warm weather makes it much harder to keep a fermenting beer at a stable temperature. A fast fermenting beer also ran the risk of acquiring characters that cause giddiness, vomiting, and in one infamous case, diarrhea.

In May, 1855, a Melbourne brewer named Murphy supplied the beer for a ball held by Victorian Governor Sir Charles Hotham in honour of the Queen's Birthday.

But the beer didn't go down too well at all. In fact, it went down but then came out again very quickly. It caused stomach cramps and led to people rushing to the toilets while trying to clench their butt cheeks to stop an early departure. The party was a "storm of indignation, disgust, and diarrhea", according to the *Melbourne Herald* at the time.

And from *The Age*, "People never tasted such bad wine and such execrable beer before. Murphy's 'entire' [aka beer] is now in utter disrepute. Murphy himself is a ruined man. No man who got a pannikin of his beer at Toorak will ever look upon it again with the eyes of mercy."

So Thomas Cooper had good reason to make a serious effort to distinguish his beer from those with the "peculiar flavour of colonial ale". Diarrhea isn't known as a strong selling point when it comes to beer – or pretty much anything for that matter.

But this isn't to say Thomas was above pulling the occasional swifty to get a questionable beer past the consumer. At times he used chillies, capsicum, ginger and honey to cover things up when the fermentation was not entirely going to plan.

"The use of ingredients such as these, and other more exotic spices and essences, was an old-fashioned method of 'improving' the ale to mask bad flavours, and make an inferior brew more presentable," the company's history *Jolly Good Ale and Old* states.

These brewing troubles led to him losing the brewery and his home – he'd borrowed money for the brewery using his mortgage as collateral. At that point he regretted giving up his milk run. And

Ann made him sleep on the lounge – once they found somewhere else to live.

After finding a new home he resumed brewing and his loyal customers – those who liked capsicum and ginger in their beers – returned to him. Despite his financial struggles Cooper only sold to private customers and refused to offer his beer to public houses. His religious beliefs caused him to avoid all contact with the public houses, which is a bit of a double standard if you ask me – he's happy to make beer but has an objection to the places that sell it. That's like an apple farmer having a moral objection to fruit shops.

Because Cooper only sold to the affluent private customer, *Jolly Good Ale and Old* opines, he allowed himself to feel a bit high and mighty because "he had not contributed to the impoverishment of the poor, who could ill afford to frequent hotels".

Thomas' descendants would have no such qualms about public houses; once the old man karked it, they started selling his beer to hotels. A practice which continues almost 150 years later, and is far more lucrative than Thomas' approach. One does wonder how Thomas would have felt about that.

EIGHT
THE JAILING OF EDMUND RESCH

These days, Resch's – best known for its pilsener (nicknamed the Silver Bullet for the silver can it comes in) – is owned by a foreign multinational SABMiller. But back in the day it was actually owned by a man whose surname sat on the can, Edmund Resch.

The man knew how to make beer – and make money. His brewery, located in the Sydney suburb of Redfern, would sell more beer than most of his rivals.

Despite being a successful businessman, and despite making beer that Sydneysiders clearly loved to drink, Resch fell victim to an appalling action during World War I. These days we may persecute people just because they belong to a certain race or religion. But there's nothing new in that – we've been doing it for years. And Mr Resch is one of many examples of this. If you're in NSW and you're drinking a Resch's maybe you should spare a thought for the injustice Australia did to the man in 1917…

In the second decade of the 21st century, the mainstream breweries in Australia suddenly started telling consumers about the history of their product. Toohey's was a big one for this – putting forward the names of founders John Thomas and James Toohey as though it was still a family company and not a brand owned by a Japanese-based multi-national who almost certainly had never had even one person named Toohey working for them, let alone two.

So, yeah, it's a bit disingenuous. And don't get me started on the breweries who decide to resurrect old brands (so they can continue to own the copyright more than anything else) but totally change the recipe so it's actually nothing like the beer it claims to be on the label. Again, it's disingenuous; it's implying some connection to history that actually isn't there. It's like buying a copy of Charles Dickens' *Great Expectations* only to find, once you start reading it, that someone else has totally rewritten it for a "modern audience". And it still says on the cover that it's *Great Expectations* by that Dickens guy.

Sorry about that digression. You got me started on that.

When it comes to historical tales, there's one that NSW brewery Resch's won't be using to promote their brand any time soon. Which is actually a bit of a pity, because it's a genuinely interesting tale; albeit a sad one that looks back on a dark period in Australian history. It's about Resch's founder Edmund Resch being jailed for committing the heinous crime of being German. Even though he'd been living in Australia for more than 50 years.

Edmund arrived in Australia in 1863 at the age of 16. After trying his hand at mining and hotel-owning, Edmund and two brothers started up a cordial and aerated waters business in Wilcannia and

Broken Hill. But Edmund really wanted to be a brewer, so he launched Lion Breweries in Wilcannia, Silverton and Cootamundra.

In 1885, after six years in business, Edmund and the brothers agreed to split up the company and each operate their own bit of it. Edmund took the Wilcannia brewery, running it until 1892 when he installed a manager and decided to retire in Melbourne. Because, let's face it, what is there for a retired person to do in Wilcannia? Except maybe die. But Resch didn't really put his feet up for long. Instead, those feet got itchy and he decided to leave Melbourne for Sydney. Maybe he never got the hang of those hook turns Melbourne people love so much. In Sydney there was a job waiting – managing a brewing, wine and spirits business that was in liquidation. Guess who ended up buying it.

Resch did. Resch ended up buying it. How could you not have worked out that one for yourself?

Known as the Waverley Brewery, because it was located in the Sydney suburb of Waverley (you may say "well, derr, with a name like that of course it was located in Waverly. But go easy big fella), it was bought by Edmund in 1897.

Three years later he bought another brewery in the Sydney suburb of Redfern and shifted the Waverley brewery to the new site. Just to confuse people trying to find the new digs, he kept the name Waverley Brewery, even though it was no longer located there (see big fella, a brewery named after a suburb doesn't always mean that's where it's located).

It wasn't until 1906 that the Resch decided to stop confusing people and removed Waverley from the brewery name and replaced it with his own. At the same time the beers started to bear his name as well. Edmund's business acumen saw the brewery outperform most others in Sydney but, as he got older and his health began to fail, Edmund handed over the reins to his Australian-born sons Edmund Jr and Arnold.

In 1913, Edmund Jr – who had been back to Germany a few times since arriving in Australia - suffered an injury to his eyes that led to him losing complete sight in one and retaining only partial vision in the other. His doctor in Sydney advised him to return to Europe for treatment, which he did.

While that may have been sound medical advice, it was really crap travel advice. Because World War I broke out while Ed Jr was in Germany and, while he managed to make it back to Australia, it was only after narrowly avoiding being interned in Germany. That was presumably because he was an Australian and Germany was at war with those pesky foreigners.

A sad irony would soon befall the Resch family. You see, while his son managed to avoid being jailed in Germany for being Australian, Edmund ended up getting jailed in Australia for being German. Somehow both sides of the World War I conflict figured the Resch family was an enemy.

And so, Edmund Sr, a frail 71-year-old man, was arrested by the Australian government in November 1917. There were no charges laid against him at the time of his arrest and he was put in an internment camp in the Sydney suburb of Holsworthy. The *Australian Dictionary of Biography* claims the arrest followed an unnamed "indiscretion" but the likely cause of his arrest was being German.

The fact he had become a naturalised citizen in 1889 did not seem to help Edmund's cause. Nor did his purchasing of several thousand pounds worth of war bonds. Or the fact his brewery was paying the difference between the military pay and previous salaries of more than 60 employees who were at the front fighting for Australia. Or even the fact that he was making beer – a job which some would likely view as the most "Aussie" job you can have short of captaining the national cricket team.

Nope, he was German. Germans were bad, so off to jail you go, sunshine.

His arrest was relatively civil; according to a *Sydney Morning Herald* report, military officers turned up at the brewery and handed him the warrant for his arrest. He then went home, had lunch and later was driven to the Holsworthy internment camp in his own car.

But the camp itself was far from civil. According to the NSW Migration Heritage Centre, the camp was overcrowded with as many as 5000 internees and was the centre that most resembled a prison.

"Heat, cold, dust, boredom, stress about families and businesses led to a malaise called 'barbed wire disease'. Guards taunted and shot at internees. Some internees suicided and others tried to escape. The most troublesome prisoners were housed in a high security gaol known as 'Sing Sing'."

Edmund was there for four months, being released in February 1918, eight months before the armistice. "It was explained by the authorities yesterday," reported the *Sydney Morning Herald* on March 1, "that the medical officers had certified that Mr Resch was in very bad health and in the circumstances the Minister for Defence had given his consent to Mr Resch's removal to his own home, where he would be permitted to remain under certain conditions."

Despite his poor health, Edmund managed to live for five more years before dying at his home in Sydney on May 22, 1923.

It should be said Edmund was not the only German brewer to suffer from the wave of racist anti-German sentiment in Australia during World War I. He wasn't even the only German brewer in his family to suffer.

His younger brother Emil was general manager of Carlton and United Breweries in Melbourne. Indeed he was one of the key figures in bringing together the six ailing breweries under the CUB name and seeing them succeed. Like Edmund Jr, Emil was in Germany at the outbreak of the war and took some time to make his way home, but when he got there he found CUB suddenly had no further use for his services and he was forced to retire.

There may have been fears within CUB of a rival spreading messages like "you wouldn't drink beer brewed by a German, would you?" but it might have also been a response to avoid criticism from the temperance campaigners. For this was around the time of the temperance movement's biggest win in Australia – six o'clock closing. Alcohol had been getting a bad rap for the last decade and pressure was building for governments to do something. For a brewery with a German-born boss, it may have seemed a way to deflect some attention by kicking him to the curb. But, as history (and chapter 14) shows, it didn't avert early closing at all.

Unlike his brother, Emil wasn't arrested and sent to an internment camp; he was able to live in his rather grand home on five hectares.

But the government felt it was not right for a German – albeit one who had become a naturalised Australian – to own so much land and so forced him to sell off two-thirds of his property. You know, because Germans were bad and all that. And because Australians can be ridiculously racist when we put our minds to it.

During World War I beer historian Brett J Stubbs says CUB would also discontinue lagers with names like Bismarck, Rheingold and Strasburg because of their German names. It would also look to downplay the Teutonic origins of lager, pointing out that Foster's – which CUB kept – was "not manufactured or sold by Germans" and was "manufactured and controlled purely by British people".

Certainly not Australia's proudest moment.

The Slab

NINE

FOSTER'S – IT'S AMERICAN FOR BEER?

Ahh, Foster's. The beer that's become a punchline in the country of its birth, while those overseas are told by Paul Hogan that it tastes like angels crying on your tongue (though, given that angels are supposed to be good and pure, making one cry would be an awful thing to do. So I'd suggest their tears wouldn't taste nice at all. They certainly wouldn't taste like a mass-produced beer. But I digress). Even people in Australia who have never tried a can of Foster's roundly mock the beer and use it as a byword for "crap". Which is a tad unfair, really. How can you call something crap if you've never tried it?

I have and, for the record, it's not too bad as mainstream beers go. Would happily choose it ahead of VB or XXXX. The original Foster's, I mean. That Foster's Classic they brought out in 2014 is ordinary.

Anyway, it's always struck me as a little funny that the rest of the world thinks Australians drink Foster's while, in reality, most of us think so little of it we wouldn't leave it out for our dog. It's perhaps the beer Australia is best known for around the world and, if you listen to the ad campaign, it's actually "Australian for beer".

What strikes me as even funnier is this iconic Australian beer – that is allegedly so Aussie that Foster's is our word for "beer" – was actually created by a pair of foreigners. And if you think Foster's is crap, then you should get a look at what Australians were drinking before it came along ...

These days, it makes sense that a lager would be the beer for a warm Australian climate. But it took a while for that stunningly obvious fact to sink in – almost 100 years after European settlement in fact.

"Australian beer was very different then to what it is now," Keith Dunstan wrote in his history of Carlton & United Brewing, *The Amber Nectar*. "It was sweet, dark, flat, heavy and warm." Mmmm, a hard-earned thirst needs a heavy, warm beer.

That monstrosity was the sort of beer that would be drunk in England, where the weather was cooler and people's taste buds gave up the fight and died a long time ago. It was not really the sort of beer that would go down well on a warm summer's afternoon in Australia.

To make a lager – as opposed to the ales Australians brought with them from the Mother Country – you need to ensure the beer is kept at cool temperatures, both during the fermentation and while in keg or bottle. For most of the 1800s that would have proved to be quite a challenge but, by 1887, two brothers named Foster were prepared to give it a go. Despite the strong connection Foster's Lager has with Australia (whether we actually drink it here or not) it wasn't actually made by Australians. Those Foster brothers were American. So blame that country for it.

William Foster and his brother Ralph left New York in 1887 and arrived in Melbourne. They had brought with them a brewer named Sieber and then got very busy setting up their brewery. Within a year the brothers had set up what was a state-of-the-art brewery for the time – including high-tech steam engines, ice-making equipment from the United States and a way of cooling a large portion of the brewery.

While there were several attempts at making lager in Australia before this time, the Foster brothers were the ones who managed to nail it – and figure out how to sell it to a public used to drinking disgusting warm beer. Their first batch hit the streets on February 1, 1899 – appearing in heavy champagne-like bottles with wire enclosures around the corks. And the fancy-looking packaging was an immediate hit. Partly because they cannily chose to launch their light, refreshing beer in summer, when thousands of thirsts needed slaking.

Another reason for the success was down to a bit of clever marketing in the form of ice from that ice-making machine they bought. If a hotel took on the Foster brothers' lager then they also got a free supply of ice to keep it cool. This ensured that anyone buying a Foster's in a hotel got a cold one and that the hotels were storing their product properly.

But the brothers' success was short-lived. Interest in lager waned during the winter of 1889 and sales slowed. A decision by the importers of European lagers to reduce their prices in order to drive the interloper out of the market certainly wouldn't have helped matters. In apparent retaliation, the Fosters beseeched the state Customs Minister to increase the duty on imported lagers, which he duly did.

In *The Amber Nectar* Dunstan suggests the Foster brothers had a more devious motive in mind when they did that beseeching to lift the import duty. They weren't doing it to protect their share of the market, Dunstan says, but rather to make their business more attractive to a buyer. For the brothers were looking to get out of the lager business. And so, two months later, they sold out to a

Melbourne group of businessmen who would go on to be a part of Carlton & United Brewing in 1907.

In the years following, the new owners would put a range of beers out under the Foster's Brewing Company name – Empire Pale Ale, Wattle Pale Ale, Harlequin Extra Stout, India Pale Ale – but only the Foster's Lager would go on to stand the test of time.

The Foster brothers themselves didn't last much longer in Melbourne. After they sold the company, they attended a few board meetings before deciding they'd had enough. They packed up and left Melbourne and precious little is known about what they did after that.

In 1891 Ralph was involved in an attempt to get a lager brewery started in Sydney but the venture never got off the ground. Then the brothers apparently headed back to the United States and nothing more was heard of the pair who gave their name to Australia's most internationally recognised beer.

That international recognition is actually relatively recent phenomenon. Before the 1970s it's doubtful many people outside Australia were drinking Foster's. There were two people largely responsible for the change, one real and one made up. The made-up one was Barry McKenzie, played by Barry Crocker in the 1971 film *The Adventures of Barry McKenzie*. In the film he is grasping a can of Foster's in almost every scene; that gave a huge PR boost for the brand, despite the film's critical panning. These days, things would be very different – no way on earth would a brewery allow their product to be associated with such a film. The real person was Paul Hogan, who was used as a spokesman for the beer in a series of ads first in the UK – where the "it's like angels crying on your tongue" saying comes from – and then in the United States, where the beer was sold in cans so big they resembled those for motor oil.

But they can't get many of us here in Australia to drink the stuff.

The Slab

TEN
STATE-BASED DRINKING

For years, it was the same. If you were a Queenslander, you drank XXXX and whatever those people south of the border drank was piss. In NSW Resch's was "the beer we drink round here" and it would be viewed as a traitorous act to quench your thirst with a beer from another state.

In Victoria, they identified with their beer so much they named it after themselves – Victoria Bitter.

South Australians had their West End, West Australians had Swan and Emu, Tasmania had their Cascade and Boag's while the Northern Territory's beer of choice was NT Draught.

Drinkers in each state would champion their own drop as though it was handed down as nectar from the Gods. If you moved states, the chances of getting the beer you used to drink in your new home was virtually nil.

But that's all in the past, yeah? There aren't any beers that are only available in their home state, right? Well, you may be surprised by this chapter ...

Walk into your local big box bottle shop and peruse the shelves and you'll be confronted with an array of offerings from loads of different breweries, some of whom didn't even seem to exist a few years ago. That's the burgeoning craft beer market for you.

But, in a way, it's not all that new. Over the years Australia has had heaps and heaps of breweries. Check out Keith Deutsher's book *The Breweries of Australia*; it's an encyclopaedic listing of every brewery that ever existed. If you discount the 40 pages at the back dedicated to the comparatively new craft breweries, there's close to 300 pages of breweries that were making beer from the early 1800s. That's an awful lot of breweries.

There was the Mulgoa Brewery, started by Gregory Blaxland – part of the team of explorers who found a path over the Blue Mountains – and his brother John and which operated from 1808 to about 1820. There was the 1840s Barwon Brewery in Geelong, which advertised itself to the "friends of temperance" as producing "a pleasant and wholesome liquor" much better for you than rum or gin. Tasmania, and not Victoria, can lay claim to the first Foster's Brewery, which was established by the unrelated Thomas Foster in the town of Glenorchy in 1832.

Way back in 1897, Thomas Gunter started up the Alice Springs Brewery due to his disgust with "brewers who drank too freely and neglected to carry out their work". The township at the time was tiny – three shops, the brewery and Gunter's hotel, with the bulk of his trade coming from travellers moving to and from the goldfields.

The town of Cooktown in Queensland had the Mt Cook Brewery, where brewer James Oddy made the popular "Tropical Beer" and where he would later end up drowning in a vat of beer because no one was around to rescue him. This was a double tragedy for the brewery as Oddy's Tropical Beer recipe died with him. Efforts by other brewers to figure out the recipe failed and the brewery ended up closing its doors.

Many of these breweries existed to serve the town in which they stood, because the further beer had to travel the greater the chance of spoilage. In a warm climate like Australia, the axiom that a beer is likely to be at its best when you can drink it while in sight of the brewery it came from definitely held true.

Many of the breweries in Australia have come and gone – and very few of them because the brewer drowned in his own creation. Some went under within a year or two simply because they made bad beer – and a lot of them did. In 1888 the *Australian Brewers Journal* described most Australian beer as "soft, tasteless, insipid, sugar-and-water sort of stuff". Others went to the wall because of bad management while those who survived for long periods would ultimately be swallowed up by a larger company and then closed down. The Australian mainstream brewing scene is very big on consolidation.

Nowadays the companies that sell beer – or any other product for that matter – want to make sure they have the biggest market possible. And so while Victoria Bitter was always the drink of the southern state and XXXX was never sighted out of Queensland, those beers and others have lost their state-based parochialism. Where once upon a time, a NSW beer drinker would insist his Toohey's was miles better than that VB piss they drink down south, these days there is no such loyalty.

You might think this sort of state-based beer is totally dead and buried. You might think that consolidation, rationalisation and globalisation has put paid to the idea of a beer only being sold within state boundaries.

You might think that — and, if you did, you'd be wrong. In what is very much a brewing throwback, every state in the country has a packaged beer that is pretty much only available there. They might even be beers you had no idea existed — and they come from one of the country's mega-brewers. While you can source these beers if you live in another state, it does involve some online ordering and delivery; you can't just walk down to the local bottlo and pick up a six-pack. Others are much harder, you have to rely on someone travelling to that state to agree to bring a few bottles back in their luggage.

So let's start off with my home state of NSW. We met the founder of Resch's — Edmund Resch — in a previous chapter. Well, the whole range of beers that bear his name — including the "silver bullet" that is Resch's Pilsener - are only available in NSW. As a New South Welshman this came as quite a surprise; because I saw Resch's beers in every bottle shop near me I figured it was the same everywhere but it's not.

The Resch family ran the brewery until 1929 when it was taken over by rival Sydney brewery Tooth and Co but the Resch name remained on the beer. Tooth in turn got swallowed up by Carlton and United in 1983 but, unlike Resch, the Tooth name or their beers did not live on. Not even the iconic KB, the initials of which stood for Kent Brewery where it was made.

Carlton and United Breweries are also responsible for a Queensland-only beer in the form of Power's Gold, a 3 per cent beer named for the former publican Bernie Power who took on

Alan Bond in the beer business - and won. In the late 1980s, Bond waded into the Queensland beer market and bought up Castlemaine Perkins, brewer of XXXX. He also managed to alienate the XXXX drinkers and open a gap for a rival brewer – enter Power's Brewing, which started in 1988 and proved a big thorn in Bondy's side. Power eventually sold out to CUB in 1993 and the big brewer apparently recognised the value of the Power's name and kept making one of his beers for the Queensland market.

In Victoria, the once-local VB is now very much a national beer. It even sponsors the NSW team in the annual rugby league State of Origin – a Victorian beer sponsoring a NSW rugby league team, who'd have thunk it? Surely, you'd think Resch's would have been a better fit. In terms of a parochial beer, Victoria's is a relative newcomer. In 2014, Little Creatures – the former craft beer pioneer now owned by multi-national Kirin through Lion – decided to launch a beer that would only be available on tap in the Geelong area and in bottles only in Victoria.

Called Furphy's Refreshing Ale, it's named in tribute to the Furphy family's foundry started in 1864 and still going today. The foundry makes stainless steel fermentation tanks of the kind used in brewing beer. The very same family's name is also where we get the term "furphy" for a false story that is claimed to be factual. The Furphy family also made water tanks emblazoned with their name and pulled by horse and cart. The carts featured in World War I, where soldiers would gather for a drink of water and a bit of a chat – from there, so the story goes, the term "furphy" came to be attached to the tall stories the soldiers told. Unless this in itself is also a furphy.

Over Bass Strait and into Tasmania there is the motherlode of parochial beers. Which is weird because it's the smallest state. Those islanders are keeping no fewer than four beers from the rest of the country. The Cascade Brewery has two in the form of a Draught and a Bitter, while fellow Apple Isle brewer Boag's has XXX Ale and Wizard Smith's (though they did send this last one to the mainland for a short stint in 2016).

Cascade has the record as the oldest operating brewery in the country. It was started by Peter Degraves in 1832, after he'd gotten out of the clink for serving five years in Hobart jail. Because he was such a nice guy, he designed plans for a new prison while in jail and gave them to the authorities free of charge.

The beer was so popular that there was a tale told of Tasmanian bushranger Nugget Brown holding up a coach and stealing a five-gallon keg of Cascade beer, leaving mailbags and valuables untouched.

Cascade have a close link to Boag's, having taken it over in 1922 but allowing it to continue to put out beers under its own name. That name on the label – "J Boag and Son" refers to two men both named James Boag. Boag Senior and Junior bought the Launceston-based Esk Brewery (named for the nearby river) in 1882, renaming it the J Boag & Son Esk River Brewery. In time people would drop the "Esk River" and the place would be known by the names of the father and of the son. Years later they were taken over by Cascade, both breweries ended up part of the Kirin stable in 2009.

In case you're wondering, Boag's Wizard Smith beer is named for a real person. Yes, his name was apparently Wizard Smith. In 1929 Launceston was submerged in a flood and old Wiz, a cart driver, saw the brewery's horses were stranded by the rising floods. So he did the right thing and saved them, earning himself a job for life from James Boag III.

Heading over to South Australia and, once upon a time, the local beer was Coopers' Dr Tim's Traditional Ale (named for the boss Dr Tim Cooper and, yes, he's an actual medical doctor). These days Coopers have sent that beer out into the world so it doesn't count as a state-based beer any more.

But West End Draught does. It takes its name from Adelaide's West End Brewery, set up in 1859 and eventually being taken over by the South Australian Brewing Company (SABC) in 1938. The West End Draught label is black and red – the colours of the SABC. Legend has it they decided on the company colours after the 1909 South Australian Aussie rules grand final. They adopted the colours of the winning team – the West Adelaide Football Club. Had Port Adelaide – the other grand finalist – won, the brewery's colours would have been black and white.

The West End Brewery continued to pump out beer until 1980, when the SABC decided to close it. Thirteen years later Lion would pick up the SABC, including the West End-labelled beers. These days West End Draught is still produced in South Australia, at a place named West End Brewery, which confusingly is a different brewery to the old West End Brewery.

For Western Australia's local beer, we look to Emu Bitter. The brewery that made it had been part of Perth for ages; it was founded in 1837, the same decade as the colony of Perth itself. It started out as the Albion Brewery, before owner James Stokes opened up a new brewery on the same site 10 years later and changed the name to the Stanley Brewery.

Shortly after the turn of the century, the business was restructured and called The Stanley Co-operative Brewery Ltd. To avoid confusion between the name of the business and the brewery itself, the latter had its name changed to its most popular beer brand – Emu.

There were several beers under the Emu name, with Emu Bitter turning up in 1923 to compete with a bitter beer from rival Swan Brewery. But they weren't rivals for much longer; in 1927 Swan bought out the Emu Brewery. Lion would later pick up Swan in 1984, when Alan Bond very much over-extended himself and had a fire sale.

There's a curious caveat to Emu's state-based credentials. While it is only available in Western Australia and the cans even advertise it as "beer for Western Australia", it's not actually brewed there. In 2014, Lion made the decision to close the Swan Brewery in the Perth suburb of Canning Vale, where Emu was brewed, and shift production to South Australia.

The last local beer on our tour around Australia comes from the Northern Territory. Well it did once – these days it comes from the CUB breweries on the east coast. Until recently, you could also get it in a bloody big bottle. Yes, this would be NT Draught, the beer that filled up the Darwin Stubby (see chapter 18) for so many years. But, CUB announced in 2015 the Darwin Stubby would be no more, which makes it exceptionally difficult for anyone other than Territorians to sample NT Draught, as the only place it's now available is on tap in the Northern Territory.

There you have it, at least nine examples of state-based beers that any self-respecting beer historian really needs to seek out before even more consolidation causes them to disappear altogether.

ELEVEN
THE CAPITAL WITH NO BEER

Canberra conjures up some odd images in most people's minds. On the one hand, they see it as an intensely boring place; a city full of politicians, public servants and main roads with no signs of life. No houses, shops or petrol stations along the roadside.

On the other hand, they would see it as the place you can buy fireworks and porn – two very lively items indeed. Regardless of your stance on either of those two consumer items, I think we can agree that boring, they are not.

When the city was being mapped out, a decision was made that would surely make it the most boring place in the country in the eyes of most Australians. That was the decision to make the nation's capital dry – yep, alcohol-free.

It was the work of one man, a politician named King O'Malley. A curious man whose name lives on in Canberra in a most curious way …

As we will see in a coming chapter, much of Australia came closer to adopting a form of the US-style prohibition on alcohol than most people realise. But there was at least one place that did ban the booze – Canberra. For the first 17 years of the Australian capital's existence, there was a legislated ban on alcohol.

This was the work of the rather unusual political figure King O'Malley, a life-long teetotaller. And, in an example of the Australian sense of humour at work, he is now best remembered in the nation's capital by a popular pub that bears his name.

O'Malley was one strange cat. He said he was never sure of his birthday – it was either July 3 or 4, 1854. He was also a member of the first Australian parliament, though he may have been there under false pretences. He claimed to have been born in Quebec, which would have made him a British citizen. But it was way more likely he popped out of the womb on his parents' farm in Kansas, which would have made him most definitely *not* an Australian citizen. And therefore most definitely *not* eligible to sit in federal parliament.

He sold insurance in his 20s but got into trouble when he began selling policies by misrepresentation. He was caught in 1888 and, shortly afterwards, fled the United States bound for Australia, where he presumably thought we'd take more kindly to crooks, given our origins. It is unclear whether there was any connection between getting busted and doing a runner but, if there was, it wouldn't be entirely surprising.

He settled in South Australia in 1895 and ran for the state House of Assembly, telling everyone "don't mind the accent. I'm actually from Quebec". A man known for speechifying and who had been prominent in the temperance movement in the United States (even though he "came from Quebec"), he carried both those traits into Australian political life.

He was elected as the member for Encounter Bay on a platform that, among other things, included ridding hotels of barmaids because he claimed they were "hired for their physical attributes rather than their prowess in drawing ale". He also called hotels "drunkeries" while alcohol was "stagger juice". He didn't much care for bartenders either, whose "knowledge extends only to the poison which they sell over their drunkery bars to the befoggled victims of their debased calling".

So, yeah, the man was no fan of alcohol.

He failed to get re-elected in South Australia in 1899, so packed his bags for Tasmania. He continued his political career there, being elected to the first federal parliament as a member for Tasmania.

In July 1901, he moved a bill that would set aside around 1600 square kilometres for a federal capital – wherever that may be, for neither the location nor the name had yet been determined. From there started a long process of working out where these 1600 square kilometres would be located. Melbourne politicians didn't want it too close to Sydney and the pollies in Sydney could do with it not being too close to Melbourne, while Queensland didn't want it too far from their border either. Places like Albury, Tumut, Bombala, Dalgety, Lyndhurst (a "blink and you miss it" spot between Bathurst and Cowra), Bathurst and Orange were among the candidates.

And the winner was … not Canberra. A ballot in 1902 was won by Tumut, with in-the-middle-of-nowhere Lyndhurst finishing second. The Sydney-based pollies hated Tumut, as it was too close to Melbourne, so they did what pollies do – knocked it back. The Senate rejected the decision, sending it back to the House for another go.

O'Malley, as Minister for Home Affairs, was effectively in charge of finding a capital location. For a time, he liked the idea of it being at Bombala, which was quite a ways inland from Merimbula on the NSW south coast and surrounded by other towns you've probably never heard of. The reason he liked it? It was cold there. "The history of the world shows that cold climates produce the greatest geniuses," the odd fellow said.

A second ballot was held in 1904 and the winner … still wasn't Canberra. This time Bombala got the vote (and if someone down there isn't selling T-shirts saying "Bombala – almost the nation's capital" then a marketing opportunity has gone begging). There was a third ballot and yep, Canberra still didn't win – the Dalgety site got the nod.

But still, the politicians weren't happy, which was good for Canberra – which, keep in mind, still didn't actually exist yet. It allowed the site to finally come under consideration in 1907, though acting Prime Minister John Forrest wasn't too pleased with the area. For him it was full of "nothing of particular importance in either scenery or great natural features." Some would say little has changed.

All the time these shenanigans were going on the parliament was located in Melbourne, which would go a long, long way to explaining why the politicians – at least those from the southern city – seemed in no great hurry to set up the new capital elsewhere. In October 1908, parliament had yet another ballot (at least the fifth, if you're keeping score) on the location of the capital. After nine rounds, with the losing town removed from the ballot at the end of each round, Canberra beat out Dalgety – partially due to fears the latter was so cold that one winter would kill the older parliamentarians. Perhaps having had enough of the mucking around by now and wanting the whole issue to be done with, the Senate passed the bill and Canberra became the location for the capital.

Work started on the capital in 1913 when, in March of that year, O'Malley drove the first survey peg into the ground. But by this time, O'Malley had already ensured the capital would be alcohol-free, drafting legislation in December 1910 to ban licences to sell liquor in the Federal Capital Territory. Yes, that's right, he banned alcohol sales in a city that hadn't even been built at that stage. He *really* hated alcohol.

But here's the thing – the law only stopped the *sale* of alcohol in Canberra; it wasn't illegal to possess beer, wine or spirits. Which was great news for the grog shops in Queanbeyan, just across the border in NSW. Canberra residents would flock to pick up booze and return to their "dry" territory. According to the National Archives of Australia, the practice was so rife that by the 1920s "around 70,000 bottles were collected every six months from those who brought alcohol back to the territory".

It was far from a secret either, a 1926 guide to Canberra, likely meant for public servants new to the city, stated "bootlegging is not necessary in Canberra, when you only have to drive across to Queanbeyan and carry back all you want … you can bring it in cartloads as long as you buy it outside the territory". Also, if you wanted a good night out, well, you went over to Queanbeyan.

Oddly enough, even that March day in 1913 when O'Malley banged in that survey peg wasn't dry – that day's grand event included a drinks list that boasted champagne, sherry, claret, port, "colonial ales" whisky and brandy. Presumably O'Malley drank water that day.

The sales ban on alcohol remained in place until 1928 when the locals voted it out in a referendum. The referendum was likely held for several reasons; firstly the workers were carrying on in Queanbeyan and giving Canberra a bad name and, secondly, the population was gradually changing from one of workers building the city to people living in it.

The biggest reason, however, was the 1926 plan to include a bar in parliament house. The pollies realised it wouldn't have been a good look to allow themselves to drink in Canberra but not the greater population.

Today, there are plenty of places to go and have a beer in Canberra; one of them is in Civic, just over the lake from Parliament House. It's called King O'Malley's and a painting of the man himself hangs over the fireplace. Curiously, it's an Irish pub – which is one nationality O'Malley never claimed for himself.

TWELVE

THE BATTLE OF CENTRAL STATION

We like to think of Australian soldiers as 10-foot tall and bulletproof, as strapping sunburned men in slouch hats, as the brave heroes who would charge into a hail of bullets without a thought for their own safety. We like to see them as larrikins with a healthy disregard for authority, especially if that authority happens to be British.

We don't like to see them as violent drunkards who could go on a rampage through the streets of an Australian city, destroying property, stealing from businesses and threatening the citizens. Because the idea that Australian soldiers are actually human, and susceptible to the same flaws as the rest of us doesn't fit with the image of them as superheroes we've built up over the years.

Which is a pity, really, because there were Australian soldiers who did incredibly brave things on the battlefield. And the valour they showed is actually amplified when we consider them to be ordinary human beings, when we consider them to be just like us. Which is what they were.

But some soldiers didn't wait until they made it to a battlefield in a foreign land to begin fighting. Some started their fighting at home – and one of them died ...

During World War I, thousands of Australian men died in the fields and towns of countries far away – Gallipoli, The Somme, Fromelles, Verdun. Most of them remained there, their bodies lying under a white cross bearing their name and rank.

But at least one soldier died in battle before he ever set foot on foreign soil. Private Ernest William Keefe – just 20 – would die, not on any of those World War I battles remembered by so many Australians, but rather at a battle remembered by so few. It was a battle that took place on a platform at Sydney's Central station and it saw Private Keefe shot and killed.

It was the awful end to an ugly day, where thousands of angry soldiers left their training camps to protest the treatment they were receiving. But it very quickly became a drunken riot. It's a story that doesn't appear in many history books, most likely because the image of soldiers getting drunk and smashing up a city doesn't gel with how we like to think of the Diggers. But it did happen – and at the end of that day one of the rioting soldiers would be shot dead – not on a foreign land but in his own country by one of his own countrymen.

It occurred on February 14, 1916, in a training camp in the western Sydney suburb of Casula, near Liverpool. Despite it being Valentine's Day, these soldiers' thoughts weren't of hearts and flowers and love but of anger and frustration.

Their anger had been brewing for some time; they were already living in overcrowded conditions and next to a prison camp for enemy aliens, where the inmates seemed to have better living quarters than the soldiers. Then there was the difficulties in getting leave and being denied the chance to have a wet bar where they could buy alcohol.

These frustrations festered and the straw that broke the camel's back was the order on February 14 that their training would be extended by four and a half hours to 40.5 hours. The soldiers had had enough and went on strike at about 9am, some of the ringleaders going from tent to tent and pulling people out.

News reports at the time claimed as many as 5000 soldiers left the camp that day in protest and marched to Liverpool, where the Light Horse training camp was. At that camp was one Private Ernest William Keefe and he and many of his fellow troopers – estimates went as high as a further 10,000 – joined the strike action. Though evidence at the coronial inquest put the figure at just over 1000.

Things got messy in Liverpool, where the soldiers set to drinking the town dry. Police Sergeant Denis Coates was stationed there and would later describe to the coroner the behaviour of some of the soldiers as very riotous. Here's how the *Sydney Morning Herald* reported the Sergeant's evidence to the coroner.

"They broke ranks and rushed the bar of the Railway Hotel, and took £140 worth of liquor from the bar. They broke a plate glass window, and rolled casks of beer into the street and consumed the contents. They then went to the Commercial Hotel, broke open the doors, removed all the liquor from the bar, and then went into the cellar and removed the beer casks to the street, and wasted what they could not consume … A large number, most of whom were half drunk and carrying bottles, went to the train."

From 1pm, full of booze and anger, the soldiers started jumping on trains at Liverpool station and heading to the city. After the first trains carrying the soldiers arrived at Central at 2pm, the soldiers formed rank and marched down George Street in a semblance of a protest, one of them carrying a placard that read "strike – we won't drill 40½ hours". More trains full of soldiers pulled in at Central and they joined the loosely organised protest – by 3pm there were as many as three thousand troopers in the city. Most of them, quite drunk and not at all interested in protesting.

Along the march, soldiers would break off from the pack to raid local hotels, commandeer citizens' vehicles and vandalise any store with a German-sounding name. The German Club in Phillip Street had its windows smashed, Kleisdorff's tobacconist was wrecked, with soldiers stealing boxes of cigars.

The march reached Circular Quay, where the soldiers turned around and had a smoko once they reached the Domain gates. After the break, they wanted some beer, so they charged the Assembly Hotel, opposite police headquarters. The cops turned up and engaged in a street battle to get them out. Other soldiers headed to Toohey's Brewery on Broadway or to Eddy Avenue. Along the way, any pub was fair game – if it was open they raided it. If it was closed, they smashed the windows and gained entry. "If all the beer in Sydney had been buried in stone vaults at the moment that the human tornado struck the city," *The Bulletin* wrote, "it would have stood a big chance of being torn from its place of seclusion."

During the afternoon and early evening, policemen were able to arrest rioting soldiers and jail them. But just after 5pm, a large number of their fellow troopers – some armed with lead pipes – turned up outside the Regent Street police station, demanding their release. Elsewhere in the city, at the Queen Victoria Building, a mob ran around frightening the public by firing their guns and overwhelming the few police officers at the scene.

"Luckily the mounted police arrived and dispersed the crowd," reported the *Sydney Morning Herald* the next day, "some of whom made towards Elizabeth Street, while others went down George Street. Many women took refuge in the grounds of St Andrews Cathedral, and from behind railings watched the mob rush past."

Through the evening one strategy was to round up the rioters and push them towards Central, in the hope they would board the trains out of the city. Also waiting there was the army's Lieutenant-Colonel Marcus Logan with 150 men. They arrived there at 8.45pm and Lt Logan told his men that as these rioters were still their comrades, they should use the butts of their rifles rather than the bayonets.

After 9.30pm the rioting soldiers began flowing into the station and began milling around the eastern archway. This included Private Keefe, who Lt Logan said he cautioned to leave several times. Keefe declined, tapping his breast pocket and saying "I've got enough here to give me permission to remain". Keefe's mother Kate would later tell the coroner that he had a revolver with him in camp so he likely had with him that night.

By 10pm the rioting troops' numbers were great enough to press their hand against the military picket. They ignored the call to move to the departure platforms, so the picket charged the mob, knocking down several rioters.

The mob responded by throwing metal rails, stones and bottles at the armed soldiers; then finding a fire hose and turning it on the picket. One witness told the coroner Private Keefe was seen wielding the hose.

"There was one continual fight," Lt Logan told the coroner. "Three of my men had been knocked insensible by bottles and one was kicked by a civilian. It was a wild fight and you could not distinguish anyone."

The picket gained control of the fire hose and used it on the mutineers. Lt Logan then gave his men the order to load their weapons, telling then to aim low if they had to fire. "Two or three shots passed between the pickets," Lt Logan said. "The pickets saw a man on one knee firing. It was Keefe that was firing. The picket in self-defence fired. We fired about 25 shots and the crowd cleared out."

Except for Private Keefe, who fell to the ground. A police constable carried him to the refreshment room, where he died. His revolver was never recovered. Government medical officer Dr Arthur Aubrey Palmer told the coroner there was "an entrance wound of a bullet on the right cheek, above the angle of the mouth. The lower jaw was fractured in front, and the tongue was much lacerated; the left, internal jugular vein was torn. The bullet passed out the lower part of the left side of the neck, and then entered the left shoulder, fracturing the collarbone and shoulder blade."

Keefe didn't die on the battlefield of Gallipoli, The Somme or the Western Front. Instead, Keefe's war ended before it even began – on the floor of a Sydney train station.

Of the surviving soldiers, 279 were discharged from the army over the riot, 36 were convicted in state courts and the ringleaders sentenced to five years in jail. Some remained in the army and ended up seeing action on the Western Front.

As for Private Keefe, despite never seeing battle on foreign soil –

and despite being killed while taking part in a riot – his name does appear on the Roll of Honour at the Australian War Memorial.

Coroner Gates exonerated Lt Logan and his men, calling the shooting "justifiable". "No doubt the deceased prominently identified himself with the mutinous and riotous soliders," Coroner Gates said, "and it was while the deceased was taking part in a most serious riot which culminated in revolver shots being fired by the rioters that he met his death."

The riot would also go on to provide some very valuable ammunition for the temperance movement. In June 1916, just four months after the drunken riot, the people of New South Wales voted in favour of pubs closing at 6pm – a law that would remain in place for almost 40 years.

The Slab

Easter Egg #2

Peter Burn scored the unfortunate historical footnote of being the first white man to be killed by Aboriginal people – at least as far as we know. There were suggestions they had killed other white settlers but they could have just as easily died after being lost in the bush. With Burn, there was a survivor who witnessed what happened. And it would never have happened without beer. See, the crime Burn committed that saw him sentenced to transportation was the theft of a 36-gallon barrel of beer. If he doesn't steal that beer, then he doesn't get sent to Australia and have his head seriously dented and his body poked with spears.

Burn found himself dead not long after he and fellow convict William Ayres wandered off looking for sarsaparilla herb, used as a substitute for tea. The pair walked a few kilometres from Sydney Cove and, cut off by rugged bush, they were set upon by a number of Aboriginal men.

Ayres managed to make it back to the tiny settlement on the coast, with a spear wedged into the skin between his shoulder blades. He was perhaps not too pleased with Burn, who ran off when Ayres was speared. That may have been a mistake on Burn's part, for Ayres was the survivor – he said he saw Burn captured by the natives before they apparently bashed him in the head and dragged him off.

Burn was never seen again; days later a soldier found remnants of his shirt pierced by numerous spear-holes, in an Aboriginal humpy.

The Slab

THIRTEEN
BANNING BOOZE IN AUSTRALIA

When we think of banning alcohol, of prohibition, we think of the United States of America. This was the place of the Great Experiment, where some bright sparks figured, if we banned alcohol, the country would be so much better and nothing bad will ever happen. Even our jails would be empty (yes, anti-alcohol proponents actually thought that would happen. Funny then, that prohibition actually created a whole new wave of crime – including organised crime).

Now it might seem that it makes sense that it would be the US that banned alcohol. After all, what else would you expect from a nation founded by Puritans? Australia, on the other hand, we were founded by convicts, larrikins and rabble-rousers. People who knew how to have a good time – no way would we have banned the booze.

Well, we didn't. But we got a whole lot closer than you may realise …

It still surprises me a little that the United States actually banned alcohol for 13 years from 1920 to 1933. I say "a little" because I know Americans in the years leading up to Prohibition were drinking a stupid amount of hard liquor – many times more than what they knock back today. On that level I understand why some would look to ban booze.

But on another level it seems such a dangerous move, economically speaking. Take a look around at how many alcohol-related businesses there are. There are bars, clubs, bottle shops big and small, distributors, breweries, wineries, distilleries and more. As well as making money for their owners, they all employ people - people who pay taxes, people who buy things and keep the economy running.

Now imagine a government forcing all those businesses to close, because it's been decided that their products, which used to be totally legal are now against the law. With a stroke of a pen, the government has suddenly thrown hundreds of thousands of people out of work. It just seems like an exceptionally bone-headed decision.

Australian politicians, while oft-considered boneheaded by the voters, were never actually so boneheaded as to turn the nation dry. Which isn't to say it didn't come close. For you see, in the late 1800s, a sizeable segment of Australia was caught up in the very same wave of temperance that swept the United States, Great Britain and other western countries. As we shall see in an upcoming chapter, six o'clock closing was an example of the power the temperance movement had – they were able to get the laws changed in several states. But how close did we really come to being a dry country? Well, several states put it to a vote and let the public decide. Not sure we can get much closer than that.

According to Ross Fitzgerald and Trevor L Jordan's *Under the Influence* (an essential book for the beer geek with a historical bent) it took about 50 years after the arrival of the convicts for Australians to start railing against alcohol. By the 1830s Australia saw the emergence of temperance societies which were, in their own way, egalitarian as they wanted to rid the country of the rich man's wine just as much as the poor man's beer or cheap spirits. But these campaigners showed a shocking lack of knowledge about the English language for, despite "temperance" meaning "moderation", these groups wanted booze in all its forms totally banned.

And these anti-alcohol campaigners started to have an effect - for instance, in the 1860s the Cricketers Arms Hotel in Victorian town of Cobden went out of business when the local cricketers took the pledge to abstain from all forms of alcohol.

By the 1880s, things had really picked up speed; the NSW Alliance got 24,000 pledges, as many as in the previous 25 years. Though it pays to be slightly skeptical of these figures as they could include children pledging not to touch a drop when they grew up. In 1885, the US-based Women's Christian Temperance Union, which laid much of the groundwork for Prohibition in the United States, set up branches in five states in Australia. This decade also saw Australian schoolchildren reading about temperance in the classroom.

Some temperance campaigners put their money where their mouth was. Looking for a replacement for the pub and hotel, they came up with the coffee palace, where caffeine replaced alcohol. These coffee palaces were all the rage in the 1880s and some of them were truly massive – one such palace had 154 bedrooms, six sitting rooms and seven bathrooms. The Federal Coffee House, built in Melbourne for the opening of the 1888 International Exhibition, sounded like a palace in more than just name. Here's how journalist Keith Dunstan described it.

"It had seven floors, an iron-framed domed tower, accommodation for 400 people with the ground and first floors given over to dining, lounging, smoking, writing, sitting and billiard rooms. It had its own ice plant in the basement, it had six 'accident proof' lifts, gas light on all floors and even electric bells."

For the coffee palaces, it wasn't a case of 'build it and they will come' for many of them did not see out the 1880s. They would close down due to lack of custom and some of them, with an undeniable sense of irony, would return to being pubs.

However, the failure of the coffee palaces did not then signal the end of the temperance movement. No, that movement was made of much sterner stuff – religion. Many of the temperance groups had a Christian leaning, which caused them to do a bit of weaseling to explain away all those references to wine in the Bible, according to Fitzgerald and Jordan.

"... temperance advocates sometimes explained away the references to alcohol by insisting that the Bible referred to two types of wine. The good wine that St Paul recommended to Timothy was unfermented, and the bad wine that [King] Solomon declared a 'mocker' was fermented."

Which is, of course, total bullshit from the temperance movement.

To give you an idea of the level of antipathy towards alcohol, I bring to your attention the work of very successful Melbourne businessman EW Cole. He built the massive Cole's Book Arcade in Melbourne and published the legendary Cole's Funny Picture

Books. He also used his position to rail against alcohol, writing a book called *The Evils of Drink Traffic*. It was a book he distributed to soldiers heading off to World War I. An extensive quote from that book might shed some light on the temper of the times.

"Intemperance cuts down youth in its vigour, manhood in its strength, and again its weakness. It breaks the father's heart, bereaves the doting mother, extinguishes natural affection, erases conjugal love, blots out filial attachment, blights parental hope, and brings down mourning age in sorrow to the grave. It produces weakness not strength; sickness not health, death not life. It makes wives widows, children orphans, fathers fiends, and all of them paupers, and beggars. It feeds rheumatism, nurses gout, welcomes epidemics, invites cholera, imports pestilence and embraces consumption. It covers the land with idleness, poverty, disease and crime. It fills your jails, supplies your alm houses and demands your asylums. It engenders controversies, fosters quarrels and cherishes riots. It crowds your penitentiaries and furnishes the victims for your scaffolds. It is the life-blood of the gambler, the ailment of the counterfeiter, the prop of the highwayman and support of the midnight incendiary."

But that's only the half of it, because Mr Cole still had not finished playing the blame game.

"It countenances the liar, respects the thief and esteems the blasphemer. It violates obligation, reverences fraud and honours infamy. It defames benevolences, hates love, scorns virtue and slanders innocence. It incites the father to butcher his helpless offspring, helps the husband to massacre his wife, and aids the child to grind the parricidal axe. It burns up and consumes women, detests life, curses God, and despises heaven. It suborns witnesses. Nurses perjury, defiles the jury box and stains the judicial ermine. It bribes voters, disqualifies votes, corrupts elections, pollutes our institutions and endangers our Government. It degrades the citizen, debases the legislators, dishonours the statesman and disarms the patriot. It brings shame not honour. In cholera and

all epidemics the liquor drinkers are the first to die."

Ahh, yes, alcohol. Anything bad that happens, it was all your fault.

Now there was no doubt the temperance campaigners were full of passion (and perhaps lacking in commonsense). But getting people all whipped up and deciding to take the pledge to never drink alcohol wasn't really cutting it. They needed to make sure those who did not want to join them couldn't get a drink anyway.

This first step along the road of legislation took the form of the local option laws which would not be total prohibition but was most definitely a step in that direction. These laws would allow people in a certain area to vote on how many licensed premises were permitted - all the way down to zero.

Local option was developed by the UK temperance movement in 1853 and its Australian counterparts jumped on it and started campaigning for it to become law here. And they kept campaigning through the 1860s, 1870s and 1880s – the anti-alcohol brigade were nothing if not dedicated. But that dedication paid off because, by the 1890s Western Australia was the only colony without some form of local option. The law varied from one colony to the next. Victorians could reduce the number of hotels to one for every 500 inhabitants while South Australia, NSW and Tasmania gave ratepayers the right to veto any new licenses being granted.

But the only people who could cast a vote were ratepayers - and that effectively meant men. And given that most men were decidedly not on the side of the temperance movement any local option votes were likely to go down. Largely driven by women, the temperance movement became an advocate of women's rights, because it was one of the few campaigns where women were able to speak in public. In fact, before the Women's Christian Temperance Union in Australia, it was rare to hear a woman speak in a lecture hall. So, to get the numbers in local option polls, the movement added granting the right to vote to women into their platform.

Their push was ultimately successful – between 1895 and 1908 every state gave women the right to vote – and they got the right federally in 1902. And, with that, the prohibitionists were in with a real shot. Seeing alcohol – and the brewers and suppliers – as the problem and the drinker as the preyed-upon victim, they saw a total booze ban as a sure-fire way to solve the booze problem.

The local option laws weren't the back-door way to prohibition the movement hoped – in no electorate did enough votes flow in to make for a dry district. But World War I did give them their biggest victory to date – six o'clock closing. In the early 1900s, it was just shops that had to be closed by 6pm but the campaigners pushed for it to be extended to hotels. In 1915, South Australians voted via referendum to extend the law to cover hotels, and Victoria, NSW and Tasmania followed suit a year later. The other states went for a more mild option - Western Australia closed the pubs at 9pm and Queensland at 8pm.

With six o'clock closing the anti-booze lobby figured it was only a matter of time before prohibition would be accepted by the average person. The news of the United States passing the Volstead Act in 1918 only made them more excited. But their hopes were to be crushed in a series of referenda held in each state through the 1920s and 1930s.

"No state in Australia ever went dry," Jordan and Fitzgerald wrote, "nonetheless, a substantial minority supported statewide prohibition during this era. Victoria received the largest prohibition vote (42 per cent) in March 1930. In other states, around a third of the electorate voted 'yes'. Tasmania, however, showed such a small voter turnout that there was some doubt as to the validity of the poll."

While the idea of prohibition effectively died in the 1930s, local option laws stayed in place in several areas. At least one area saw it keep operating for almost a century. This wasn't in some hicksville area of the country where they have dirt roads and no electricity either - it was just over 10km west of the Melbourne CBD.

Until May 2015, about half of the municipality of Boroondara was officially recognised as a "dry zone". Farcically, the border between wet and dry went right down the middle of the street in some cases. Such as Burke Road, where you have to cross the road to get a beer.

Seems a three-fifths majority voted for the area to be dry way back in 1920 - and it just stayed that way until 2015. What the dry area meant was residents there got to vote on whether to issue any new liquor licences – mainly to restaurants. The ballots – costing upwards of $9000 each time – were once conducted via polling booths but in the latter years, switched to postal votes. And yes, residents could be fined for not voting.

"The original 1920 dry boundary held strong for more than 30 years," Ian Rose wrote in *The Age* in 2013.

"The first establishment to break the booze ban was the venerable Box Hill Golf Club ... The golf club's historical 'yes' vote and the means by which they won it in 1956 have become a part of local mythology. The story goes that, in order to satisfy the requirement for licence applicants to invite objections to their

bid through advertisement, the golf club craftily put an ad in a Mildura weekly newspaper, as far from Melbourne as state boundaries would allow."

Rose found out that wasn't actually true – an announcement was published in a Melbourne newspaper.

The local option polls in Boroondara weren't exactly a rubber stamp either. According to the *City Journal* in 2013, out of the 47 polls since 1990, 36 licences were approved, but 11 knocked back. It appears the populace cared less and less as time wore on - the last licence was knocked back in 2004. Much to the dismay of Mary Drost, a member of BRAG (Boroondara Residents Action Group).

"Everybody always used to say no," Mary told *City Journal*'s Simon Love in 2013, "but new people are moving in and they've got different ideas. Things change. Which is a pity."

For the last few years of its existence, the local council had been pushing the state government to remove the law requiring residents to vote, citing the cost of each ballot. In May 2015, Victorian Commission for Gambling and Liquor Regulation finally agreed and took over the role of deciding on licenses.

The Slab

FOURTEEN
SIX O'CLOCK CLOSING

These days, the argument around pub closing hours is that they're open way too late. And, you ask me, I reckon there's some level of logic there. I mean, really, who needs to be able to get a drink at 3am? Or needs to be able to get into a licensed club at 6am? Sure, I'm a cranky old man who has been asleep for hours by the time the clock says 3am but still, it's too late to be looking for more alcohol.

It was an argument that several states in Australia didn't need to bother with for almost half a century. Because around World War I they said, "pubs are closing at 6pm. Deal with it." And everyone did. Sort of. They didn't drink any less; for a while they were drinking the same amount as before when the pub was open until 11pm. Then, it was like they got better at it and worked out how to drink more in that one hour than they used to knock back in five or six.

Everyone hated it except for two groups of people usually at opposite ends of the spectrum – the temperance movement and the hotel owners. The former loved it because they thought they'd shut down the pubs while the latter loved it because they made more money in one hour than they used to when they opened until 11pm …

It'd be safe to say that no single thing changed the beer-drinking landscape in Australia more than six o'clock closing. It completely changed the look of hotels, some of those changes are still with us today. In the early 20th century most hotels only had a small bar where they could serve their customers. Early closing started the transformation of the bar into a steadily growing beast to offer more and more space for men to lean against while calling for a last beer before the little hand hit six.

Tables and chairs were cleared out because leisurely drinking was no longer the order of the day. Instead, it was all about "vertical drinking", standing upright and getting as many into you as quickly as possible. No time to sit and relax. Besides, no furniture meant the publican could squeeze in a few more paying patrons. Things like pool tables and dartboards were thrown out the back too, and tiled floors and walls began to pop up so as to make it far easier to clean up at the end of that torrid hour between the men's knock-off time and 6pm.

It set the scene for what would become the six o'clock swill; horrendous scenes of men getting as many beers into them in a short space of time, men pissing against the bar so as not to waste valuable drinking time in the toilet, men pushed out the door with their stomachs full of beer and nothing else – at least until some of them threw up in the streets. This bingeing pattern of drinking would arguably create lasting impacts on the way generations of men viewed alcohol; as something to down as fast as possible so you get drunk rather than drink responsibly and pace yourself.

It would also come to usher in the bottle shop. Before six o'clock closing people would buy a takeaway bottle of beer or two over the bar and that was fine with everyone. But over time, with a teeming mass of men pushed up against the bar aching for a drink, some bloke looking for a few bottles was just taking up space and chewing up the bar staff's limited serving time. The drinkers hated him, and the bar staff hated him, and so bottles came to be purchased at a space within the hotel dedicated to that purpose. A space that would, over time, become the bottle shop.

Early closing also gave organised crime a leg-up – though not on the scale of Prohibition and the Mafia in the United States. Early closing in Australia saw a return of the sly grog trade, not seen since the Gold Rush era. Despite the dull and boring temperance party's hopes and dreams, people didn't stop drinking at 6pm. They still wanted more booze, or at least to drink at the same rate they did before six o'clock closing, and so the criminal element were only too happy to help them out.

Sometimes it was at via the hotel back door, where the publican would slip a few bottles into the arms of a valued customer. Sometimes it was a trestle table set up in a laneway with some unlabelled bottles set up and someone on the corner to watch out for the cops. Sometimes it was in a private home set up specifically as a liquor joint for those in the know. In Sydney Kate Leigh was the sly grog queen and she owned a house that was used for this purpose, as well as renting rooms in the backs of grocery and fruit shops to sell to the locals. They weren't poorly stocked places either; she bought her beer in bulk, direct from breweries like Tooth's and Reschs and Johnnie Walker whisky from the wholesalers. The cops raided one of Leigh's places in the suburb of Surry Hills in May 1943. According to a news report of the court case, the cops looked under the floorboards and found 1001 bottles of beer, 84 bottles of whisky and one bottle of wine.

The sly grog trade also increased violence in the inner city of Sydney as standover men sought to steal the ill-gotten gains of the sly groggers and the sly groggers in turn hired their own muscle to keep their money safe.

In a great many places around the nation, a person didn't even need criminals to supply their booze for them. In rural areas, where farm workers had no chance in hell of knocking off in time to get a few drinks before 6pm, the pubs stayed open later and the cops turned a blind eye as long as everyone behaved. According to academic Tanja Luckins many pubs in Tasmania and even in the cities of Melbourne and Sydney just didn't bother closing up at 6pm. Also, those hotels with a meals permit could stay open until 8pm – and it doesn't take a genius to figure out there wasn't a whole lot of eating being done in those dining rooms.

Ironically, just about the only thing it didn't change was the amount of beer we drank. Statistics show there was little change in the drinking levels before World War I and afterwards. Indeed, as six o'clock closing wore on, we actually ended up drinking *more*, not less.

The idea that hotels should close at 6pm came out of early closing acts that governed other shops in the various states. Temperance advocates argued, if the butcher and the baker had to close their doors at 6pm, the pubs should too. Which seems a hard point to argue – in the early 20th century, pubs were open for a very long time indeed. They swung their doors open at 5am or 6am and kept them open until around 11.30pm.

Still, for the first decade and a half, the push for early closing of hotels didn't gather much momentum. Partially due to an inability from campaigners to agree on a time – they might want anything from 6pm to "not quite as late as they're open now". It was South Australia that got the six o'clock closing ball rolling, when it held a referendum on March 27, 1915, offering voters a choice of every hour between 6pm and 11pm. Perhaps not reading the wind, the pub owners ignored compromising with a call for 9pm while the temperance movement put its weight behind 6pm. The latter won the day with 57 per cent of the overall vote and six o'clock closing in South Australia became law in March 1916.

The temperance movement in the other states took note of that and began pushing for their own early closing. Victoria was next, where the politicians, fearful of putting it to a public vote, passed legislation in July that brought forward hotel closing to 9.30pm – the law coming into effect in July 1915. And everyone seemed quite happy with that.

But then NSW Premier William Holman went and buggered everything up. In September 1915, the NSW Legislative Assembly had decided that 9pm was an acceptable closing hour – largely to stave off the high probability the public would vote for 6pm if they were asked for their opinion via a referendum. The temperance movement was happy with the government giving in principle support for 9pm and was willing to wait for the legislation to be put forward.

But then Premier Holman had a brain explosion. In October 1915 he put forward legislation that included 10pm closing. The temperance movement went, "okay, now it's on like Donkey Kong" and they developed a single-minded focus on 6pm closing. Not that Holman cared, at least until leading temperance campaigner Albert Bruntnell convincingly won a byelection for a state seat.

That – and the fear of being punted at the next election – convinced Holman to announce a referendum on the issue would be held on June 10, 1916. Across the state of NSW 62 per cent voted for 6pm and 9pm closing got 32 per cent. Eleven o'clock closing got less than 1 per cent of the vote.

Around the same time Tasmania also voted for 6pm closing. And so with three states adopting six o'clock closing Victorians started to think their earlier deal of 9.30pm was no longer quite so good. So they pushed for 6pm too and, the government, knowing when it was beaten (and possibly cursing the boneheaded machinations of NSW Premier Holman) conceded defeat and joined the six o'clock club.

That longtime bastion of conservatism that is Queensland bucked the trend and never brought in six o'clock closing. The state stuck to its guns and left opening hours alone until 1923, when it brought in 8pm closing. Western Australia paid no attention to what was happening elsewhere and opted for 9pm closing.

The move is often seen through the lens of wartime sacrifice, of not wanting to enjoy yourself at home while Australian soldiers were dying overseas. But that's not really true; World War I came and went but those six o'clock closing laws stayed in place. The island state of Tasmania was the first to wake up to itself and put an end to six o'clock closing. In 1937 – 19 years after the war – it moved the hours back to 10pm. The NSW public took a whole lot longer to come around. Ten years after Tasmania ditched six o'clock closing, NSW held a referendum where voters decided to stick with 6pm. But, by the time of another referendum was held in 1954, the vote was narrowly in favour of 10pm closing. That's 36 years after World War I finished.

Victorians would have to wait another 11 years to throw off the shackles of six o'clock closing. South Australia – the first state to introduce it – would also be the last to revoke it. Those guys waited until 1967 – almost a half-century after the Armistice that ended World War I.

After the end of six o'clock closing in each state, the hotels underwent another change. People could now linger in pubs, so the tables and chairs came back. They might also want to eat something, so kitchen facilities began making an appearance. And, because the pub was no longer swimming in testosterone, piss and vomit, women decided they might go down to the local with their friends or their other half. And they wanted some entertainment too, so in came the bands, the jukebox, the pool tables and dartboards.

If you do a search for "six o'clock closing" on Google, it will return a number of pages related to the six o'clock swill as though the two phrases mean the same thing. It's not exactly Google's fault; it seems plenty of people see the phrases "six o'clock closing" and the "six o'clock swill" as the same thing, as though the swill happened from the moment the pubs started closing early. But it's more likely the swill took some time to arrive, appearing several decades after six o'clock closing was introduced, according to academic Tanja Luckins.

"Historians have tended to link the emergence of the 'six o'clock swill' to the introduction of early or six o'clock closing during the Great War. A closer analysis suggests it was not licencing law alone which impelled its emergence but historically specific conditions during World War II."

If you think about it, it make sense that the crude drinking practices associated with the swill only started appearing after World War II. Firstly, the country lost thousands and thousands of young men in World War I, which meant there were simply less men around to be crowding into hotels and drinking. Also, the nation was busy getting back on its feet after the war. Then, in 1929 came the Great Depression and money was very tight. That carried through to the late 1930s and then, in 1939, along comes World War II.

So the idea of drunken hordes swilling away their money at a hotel night after night just doesn't seem likely before World War II. The historical beer drinking stats back this up – they remain pretty consistent between the wars. Also, in a 1947 referendum, NSW voters chose to stick with six o'clock closing (more than a million compared to the 600,000 who wanted 9pm closing). If the "swill" was already widespread by this time, it's hard to see such a strong majority voting in favour of continuing it.

In fact the very phrase "six o'clock swill" doesn't seem to have become a common term before the 1940s. When you're talking about contemporary references, searching via the online newspaper archive Trove, the earliest mention I could find for "six o'clock swill" was from the *Perth Daily News* in October 4, 1944, which carried a report from Sydney about the United Licensed Victuallers Association calling for "changed drinking hours to avoid the 'six o'clock swill'." That the phrase six o'clock swill appears in inverted commas would indicate it was a new and perhaps unfamiliar phrase to newspaper readers.

Incidentally, the 1940s is also when the per capita consumption of beer starts climbing after being stable since the turn of the century (albeit with a drop during the Depression).

Also, in the book *Caddie*, the memoirs of a 1920s barmaid written with the help of Dymphna Cusack, the word "swill" never appears – an indicator the phrase wasn't in use then.

Instead, she refers to the "six o'clock rush" (a term still in use as late as 1946) described thusly;

"The first arrivals crowded against the counter, less fortunate ones called above their heads, late comers jostled and shouted and swore in an attempt to be served before closing time.

"It was a revolting sight and one that took me a long time to take for granted. The smell of liquor, the smell of human bodies, the warm smell of wine, and on one early occasion even a worse smell, as a man, rather than give up his place at the counter, urinated against the bar."

While urinating against the bar is pretty disgusting, the context shows that sort of behaviour was very much out of the ordinary at the time. In general Caddie's memoirs of the time spent behind the bar speak more of a busy period in the evenings rather than unremittingly disgusting behaviour.

Cusack also co-wrote *Come in Spinner*, published in the 1950s, which features the term "six o'clock swill" and descriptions that sound rather more familiar.

"I don't see that we can ignore any longer," one character in the novel says, "such outspoken comments as appeared in this morning's paper. And when the papers talk of 'pig-trough drinking', 'the six o'clock guzzle' and the general hoggishness of our drinking conditions, they're absolutely right."

So what happened to switch the rush to the swill? Well, the actions of John Curtin's federal government probably had something to do with it. In 1942, the cabinet cut the amount of alcohol allowed to be produced. In the April-June quarter of 1942, alcohol production was cut by 23 per cent to 7,201,000 gallons a month.

On top of this, the government restricted hotel opening hours to seven hours a day. Curtin also pressured the states to reduce hotel trading hours by another hour a day, as well as make drinking in parks illegal and exclude women from hotels.

So you have hotels open for fewer hours each day and there's less beer to go round. What do you think that might create? Perhaps a mad dash to make sure you get your share, to drink as much as possible?

I reckon it would. A *Sydney Morning Herald* journalist writing in November 1945 noted the effect war had on the city's drinking practices. While, before World War II, six o'clock closing led to "an inevitable rise in the inebriation rate", it worsened during the war.

"Now, when beer shortage – war-caused or crop-caused – is a complication, the rush hour has brought trough drinking," the journalist wrote.

Which suggests to me that events in World War II brought on the traits we have come to recognise as the six o'clock swill and that they didn't exist to that degree before that point.

FIFTEEN
THE DARWIN REBELLION

Much is made of the Eureka Stockade, where gold miners rebelled against the colonial authority of England. The miners had had enough of being forced to pay for a mining licence and then have the police constantly request to see it. They also pushed for the right to vote and own land.

As the name Eureka Stockade suggests, the miners built a stockade from overturned carts and bits and pieces of wood and waited for the troops and police to come and get them. Which they did – in about 10 minutes they punted the miners out of the stockade. There has been some suggestion that the miners had gotten smashed on sly grog the night before and weren't in any fit state for a fight to the death.

It's an event that's gone down in history as the birth of democracy in Australia, as the first real political revolt in the country. Even though it wasn't really a success by any measure. While Eureka gets all the attention, there was a very successful political rebellion in Darwin in the early 20th century and hardly anyone has heard of it. And, yes, beer plays a small part in events ...

The foundations of *The Slab* lay in the Darwin Rebellion of December 1918. It was while reading other books and finding snippets of Australian beer history that encouraged me to dig deeper and find out more about those moments. The first of those happened while reading Cyril Pearl's 1969 book *Beer, Glorious Beer!*. In that book Pearl starts off with the story of "the most successful rebellion Australia has seen" and it "was sparked off by a rise in the price of beer". He talks of an intermittent beer supply in Darwin of the early 20th century, of the government owning hotels and the simmering resentment that boiled over into a riot that ousted the Northern Territory's federally-appointed administrator. Ahh, so Australian isn't it? We love our beer so much that we're willing to riot when the price goes up.

Pearl paints the whole rebellion as sparked by beer, which simply isn't true. Such is the trouble with beer and other forms of alcohol when they crop up in our history. We tend to see it as saying something about the Australian character and so will exaggerate the significance of alcohol in the story. The Rum Rebellion is a classic example of this – it had nothing directly to do with rum and was a power struggle between William Bligh and John MacArthur. But decades afterwards some historian comes up with the catchy phrase of "Rum Rebellion" and now we all think alcohol played the starring role.

In the case of the Darwin Rebellion, beer was there, but its availability was a long way short of being the protesters' only grievance. In fact, to make it a rebellion about beer actually cheapens what is a great story – and perhaps a far better one than the Eureka Stockade.

The rebellion itself kicked off on December 17, 1918, but its roots go all the way back to 1911. That was when the Northern Territory came under the control of the federal government. Prior to that time, Territorians had been able to vote in South Australia's state elections and, since federation in 1901, the federal elections. But when the feds took over on January 1, 1911, those living in the Northern Territory lost all their voting rights. And, as history had told us time and time again, taking away people's voting rights is a surefire way of making them very cranky indeed.

Nor does it help when the government appoints some guy to be in charge of you without asking how you feel about that. Which is what happened when the feds dropped in John A Gilruth as Administrator of the Northern Territory.

Things started off hopeful for Gilruth and the locals, who figured that having the feds in charge might mean they would funnel some money towards the Territory. Gilruth did look to boost the economy, through the promotion of mining and agriculture, and the development of a meatworks in Darwin run by English firm Vesteys.

But things started to go pear-shaped with the start of World War I. The federal government had tired of the novelty of running the Northern Territory and stopped sending funds up north – because, hey, they had a war to pay for instead.

As the public face of the feds Gilruth was a lightning rod for the public's growing dissatisfaction. The man himself didn't help matters by being what one might describe as "a bit of dick". He routinely got into arguments with the trade unions, employers, workers and pretty much anyone else who got within yelling distance of him.

The newly-formed Darwin branch of the Australian Workers' Union repeatedly got under Gilruth's skin with several strikes from 1914 onwards. While most of them weren't successful, Gilruth – in his job of representing the federal government in negotiations with the AWU – looked to smash the union to pieces. Funnily enough, that didn't sit at all well with the union officials or the workers they represented.

From 1915 the AWU held several strikes over the price of beer, which did go up after the control of the hotels transferred to the government – effectively Gilruth. But these strikes didn't have any effect on the price of beer.

One of Gilruth's projects did get off the ground – the Vesteys meatworks, which opened in 1917 after several years of negotiations and planning. However, the relationship between the bosses and the workers was poor. The company brought in labour from interstate and promised them good wages but didn't deliver. With the higher cost of living in Darwin making it difficult to survive, the workers regularly went on strike to secure better pay.

So Darwin of the 1910s was a city where strikes and animosity directed at those in power were very much par for the course.

It was at the end of the war that things reached a fever pitch. Workers in the meatworks and the docks were granted time off to celebrate Armistice Day – the end of World War I. But, Gilruth, in a real dick move, refused to allow hotel workers time off. Frustrated, they took the day off anyway and, upon returning to work the next day they found Gilruth has suspended them.

A short while later, in a perfect example of not realising which way the wind was blowing, Gilruth jacked up the price of beer by 16 per cent. And so lit the fuse of the powder keg he had been sitting on for years.

On December 17, 1918, a thousand men who had totally had a gutful of Gilruth and the federal government marched on Government House in Darwin, bringing with them an effigy of the Administrator tied to a stake. Gilruth eventually came out to speak to the crowd, but only to say they couldn't make him do anything because he didn't answer to the people of Darwin. Not surprisingly, that didn't go down too well.

The hordes broke down the fences and stormed the grounds, with Gilruth jostled and manhandled as he escaped into the refuge of Government House. Then the rally organisers called for calm. And calm they got, if by calm you mean carrying that effigy of Gilruth to the gates, soaking it in petrol and setting it alight.

Throughout Christmas and into January 1919, Gilruth and his family were virtual prisoners in Government House, upon which were mounted two machine guns for protection. The whole issue worried the feds enough to send the lightly armed gunboat HMAS Una up to Darwin to offer protection for Gilruth.

In January 1919, the protesters sent a demand to the Prime Minister,

> *"We, the citizens of the Northern Territory, beseechingly implore you to recall the Administrator, Dr Gilruth, in the interests of life and property, as his autocratic administration is fast reaching a grave crisis."*

It had the desired effect; in February, the cruiser HMAS Encounter arrived to take Gilruth back to Melbourne.

Later that year - after the price of beer was lowered - a Royal

Commission was held into the rebellion. It noted the unfairness of Territorians being governed by laws over which they had no say and the poor performance of Gilruth who, "had little toleration for any person who disagreed with him, and was temperamentally unsuited for filling the office he occupied".

Harold Nelson, one of the leaders of the protest, would win the Northern Territory's first seat in federal parliament in 1922 and held it until 1934. In a small slice of irony, one of his sons would become an Administrator of the Northern Territory.

SIXTEEN

MINING BLACK GOLD FROM BREWER'S YEAST

Vegemite is the jet black spread for which Australians are known the world over. And perhaps we're also known for having a strange set of taste buds, for any time a foreigner tries the stuff, they gag, pull a face that looks like they've been poisoned and then try and find a bucket they can spit it into.

I have my suspicions that things would be different if the Vegemite was correctly applied. My theory is the foreigners see it as a breakfast spread on par with peanut butter, jam or honey and so they slather it on. We in Australia of course know that's a rookie error – no one here would eat the stuff like that. Instead, a thin spread on the toast is best; it's a strong, salty taste. No doubt you're going to hate it when you trowel the stuff on.

Something we Aussies love about Vegemite is that it comes from beer. That yeast that makes it such a strong source of vitamin B comes from breweries, after it has been used to ferment beer. Making use of a byproduct that would have otherwise been thrown away – Vegemite was into recycling long before it was cool …

If Carlton and United Breweries had been more persistent, they could well have been directly responsible for a black-as-tar breakfast spread loved by Australians and pretty much no one else. But they weren't and instead it was the Fred Walker company (which would eventually become Kraft) that stuck with their concoction made with brewer's yeast for nearly two decades before it became a success.

Yes, this is Vegemite we're talking about.

Back before the First World War, there was a bit of a market for Marmite, a British spread made with spent yeast from breweries. The war meant it was hard to get supplies from Britain to Australia (they wanted our troops but wouldn't give us any breakfast spread in return) and so local outlets looked to fill the market with their own products. But they had to work out how to make it, because the Brits wouldn't give us the recipe either.

Carlton and United had a crack in 1918 - after all, they had a plentiful supply of spent yeast they needed to do something with. If they could make some extra bucks off it, so much the better. So they launched Cubex on the market - the name presumably derived from Carlton and United's initials and the fact it was a yeast extract (bet they stayed up all night coming up with that name). The company advertised it as "better than beef tea" (which is not really that hard), and claimed it could be smeared on toast or sandwiches or added to gravy. CUB even suggested it could somehow cure skin ailments (by eating it, not by smearing it on your flesh). That's not as left-field as is sounds for, according to Keith Dunstan's history of CUB, people would queue up outside the brewery's truck entrance gate carrying billy cans, jam jars and jugs to buy some used yeast for all sorts of reasons. Dunstan also suggests it stopped because some people were using it to brew beer – which seems unlikely given the yeast would have been dead.

Despite the queues for yeast, they weren't also lining up in droves to buy Cubex. The market said "Stick to making beer, guys" and didn't buy it in hordes, and by the early 1920s, CUB gave up.

But Fred Walker, a man with a fascination for finding ways to preserve the nourishment and vitamins of foods, decided to have a go. He did a deal to purchase all of CUB's spent yeast for a year. No doubt the executives at CUB said, "hey, we managed to sell off all that yeast anyway. Cool!"

Fred wasn't about to work out what to do with that yeast himself; he hired food technologist Cyril McAlister in 1923 to work out how to make something palatable out of spent VB yeast. And if you've seen spent yeast that's no small ask.

"Barrels of yeast arrived by truck from Abbotsford," wrote grandson Jamie Callister in Cyril's biography. "The stuff was pungent, brown and bitter. When the lids were lifted the reek was ghastly - a demonic concoction of rotting compost and stale eggs. Yet through some mysterious alchemy, some trick of science, Cyril was expected to transform this foul fungal mash into a flavoursome food product that Fred Walker could proudly sell to households across the nation."

That it took him less than a year to do it is testament to Cyril's talent – and possibly his family's stomach for they were used as guinea pigs on test versions of the spread. Vegemite went on the market in 1923, the same year he was hired.

Fred Walker was so confident of success he negotiated a deal with CUB for an ongoing supply of yeast. But his confidence appeared misplaced; just like the issue CUB faced with Cubex, sales of Vegemite were poor for some time. Maybe the name was part of the problem, which prompted a short-lived switch from Vegemite to Parwill. That was a name surely driven by the marketing department, who must have been champing at the bit to use the phrase "Marmite but Parwill". And the CUB execs, went "jeez, I wish we'd thought of that". But the new name didn't work - nor did efforts to tout the vitamins in Parwill/Vegemite or the health benefits of the spread.

But Fred must have seen a rosy future for Vegemite, because he had broadened his yeast sources. In the 1930s he was also buying up to eight tonnes a week of yeast from Sydney's Tooth's brewery (though not yeast that had been used to make porter, which was apparently too bitter to be used for Vegemite).

It would take another World War to make people like Vegemite. The vitamin benefits as well as the durability of the spread impressed the government, who chose to include Vegemite in the ration kits for Australian soldiers during World War II. This led to a shortage of Vegemite at home which, in a case of absence making the heart grow fonder, created a desire for Australians on the home front for the product. After the war things really picked up for Vegemite, due to both the home country yearning for the stuff and the soldiers overseas having developed a taste for it while at war.

But the success of Vegemite wasn't good news for everyone, according to Callister's book. The factory workers began to hate the rising level of yeast deliveries.

"Customised tankers and trailers emblazoned with company logos transported 1200 gallons (5455 litres) of yeast at a time to the Vegemite section of the Riverside Avenue factory. The torrent became so great that workers complained

of yeast arriving at 'all odd hours', preventing their participation in the company's social activities. At the Sydney plant, a brewery strike that halted yeast supplies for a week was greeted with relief."

While Vegemite's key ingredient is a leftover from brewing, in 2015 there were claims the spread could be used for making alcohol. Federal Indigenous Affairs Minister Nigel Scullion claimed the foodstuff was being used in the Northern Territory and Queensland to make moonshine. There were also unsubstantiated reports people were buying as many as 20 jars at a time to make alcohol. The story exploded for a short while, with the *Media Watch* TV show criticising everyone for running the story without asking whether Vegemite can actually be used to make alcohol.

They said no and focused on the assumption that, because Vegemite features brewer's yeast, it's for that purpose it would be used. The show rightly pointed out the Vegemite yeast is dead and therefore intensely unlikely to start any sort of fermentation.

But Vegemite can be used in the process of distilling liquor, as a yeast nutrient - just google "Vegemite" and "distilling". Two scientists from the University of Queensland wrote a piece about the topic for *The Conversation* website. They tried and failed to cultivate yeast from Vegemite but did note "it still can be used as a substrate for other microorganisms that could ferment the sugars and, ultimately, produce alcohol. That's true of any sugar-containing food, including fruit and fruit juices," the article stated.

There are also a number of stories in the *Courier-Mail* newspaper that reference the use of Vegemite, as part of a "toxic" mixture that also includes ingredients like fermented fruit, sugar, and fruit juice.

A year later other researchers at the University of Queensland decided to put the matter to bed and see if Vegemite could somehow feature in the process of brewing up some sort of alcohol. And it turns out, yes it can.

Researcher Dr Ben Schulz said, yes, you can make something vaguely beer-like with Vegemite, but not if you rely on it to provide yeast. Instead, you need to add a sugar source and some yeast, the good doctor said. "And then all of those things together will make an alcoholic beverage, which at a stretch you can call beer," he said to the *Brisbane Times*.

Dr Schulz said the idea was to test the truth of the claims that Vegemite on its own could be used to make some sort of homebrew.

"The rationale for that previously was that Vegemite was a good source of yeast and you needed yeast to ferment the sugar and turn that into alcohol," Dr Schulz said.

"But we've shown that there is nothing 'alive' in Vegemite. Instead the Vegemite is a really good nutrient source, it is a really good food source for the yeast."

Where do you get yeast? Well, wild yeast is floating around in the air and you can also get it from the skins of fermenting fruits. The research found that the Vegemite homebrew would be substantially cheaper than store-bought beer, but not as tasty. Dr Shulz describes the resulting concoction as bland with a distinct Vegemite aftertaste.

SEVENTEEN
WHAT ARE ALL THE Xs FOR?

Queensland is home to the beer brought to you by the letter X. Four of them in fact. It's also the beer that spawned another "Queenslanders are stupid" gag – namely, "they gave it that name so Queenslanders could spell it". Ah, how the rest of the nation laughed. But really, beer drinkers in some of the other states can't really laugh. I mean, how hard is it to spell "VB", or "New" or "Old"?

But at least those names contain different letters, and don't resemble the name you'd get if you feel asleep in front of a typewriter and hit your head on the keyboard.

Not that that is how the beer got its name – that is in fact steeped in history. Well, sort of ....

What do those four Xs mean on the label of Queensland's XXXX Bitter? Nothing. Oh, the idea of writing Xs on beer once may have meant something in ye olden days but by the time XXXX came onto the market – and probably for a while beforehand – any meaning of an X on beer was little more than a marketing gimmick.

Apparently in ye olden days of England, a brewer would mark his barrels of strong beer with an X, for they were subject to higher taxes. There is also the suggestion that some brewers may not have been especially literate, so an X is an easier mark to make than writing "strong beer" on each barrel.

After a while the mindset of "one X good, more Xs better" seems to have grabbed hold with brewers. So they'd add another X to the beer, presumably in the hope the punters would conclude that a XX beer simply has to be better than one marked X. Even though no one actually knew how much stronger or better a beer got with each extra X. Of course, some bright spark was soon enough going to start selling a XXX beer and then that led to someone else – ie Castlemaine Perkins – selling a XXXX beer. It seems four Xs is the limit consumers set before they decided brewers were just taking the piss. Not long after XXXX came out, a rival Brisbane brewer actually tried to out-X them, by releasing a XXXXX beer. It seems the public went "come on guys give it a rest". Which was a good thing, because it saved us from the stupidity of seeing TenX beer.

As for the beer itself, it likes to put a parochial foot forward and declare itself the "Pride of Queensland", as it so very modestly states on their longneck labels. While the XXXX Bitter beer was born in Queensland, the Castlemaine Perkins brewery that makes the beer has its origins in another state altogether.

The "Castlemaine" in the name, according to Keith M Deutsher's *The Breweries of Australia*, refers to the town of the same name in Central Victoria. The Fitzgerald family started up a brewery in the town, and employees moving states or forming partnerships led to Castlemaine breweries being set up in Queensland, Western Australia and NSW.

The brewery in Brisbane, Queensland, came about it when two guys – Michael Quinlan and an N Donnelly joined forces to start a shipping business in 1871. Donnelly didn't hang around very long, selling his part of the business to Quinlan. In 1878 Quinlan died, passing on the business to his widow. Just before his passing, Quinlan set in motion a partnership with the Fitzgeralds at Castlemaine to establish a brewery in Brisbane.

In 1877, development of the brewery in the Brisbane suburb of Milton began, which would bear the name Castlemaine Brewery. In September the following year, the first batch of beer – XXX Sparkling Ale – was ready for sale.

The Lion website claims the XXXX trademark was born in 1878 but that seems a bit iffy as it seems that name didn't exist until 16 years after that. In his book, Deutscher said Castlemaine applied for the trademark of XXXX in 1894, but didn't use it until 1916, when an extra X was added to XXX Sparkling Ale. Because, as we've established, more Xs are better.

Around the same time a dapper man in a suit, tie, boater hat and with a very big head showed up – Mr Fourex. The mascot of sorts first appeared in a magazine ad for XXXX and would go on to be the visual representation of the brewery through to 1967. He was recognised in 2005 as one of the 12 icons of Queensland.

There are a few rumours as to who served as the model for the big-headed gentlemen. One claim is that it was the general manager at the time, Paddy Fitzgerald. But I prefer another explanation, just because it has more colour; that tale has it that the Mr Fourex model was an apparently well-known dwarf who sold newspapers in Brisbane's Fortitude Valley in the 1920s.

Mr Fourex has come in various guises over the years, some of which have fallen victim to kidnappers. In June 2004, someone managed to steal a six-metre, 45kg inflatable version of the mascot from the Ipswich Cup race day. And, in calling for his safe return, the brewery leapt at the chance for some free PR.

"An image was supplied to the police for distribution to all units to be on the lookout for him, and we're still considering filing a missing person's report," a brewery spokeswoman told the *Courier Mail* newspaper.

"Theres nothing they can do with him without the generator and they'd have to have a pretty big house to display him in."

The brewery offered a 40-case reward for his safe return, and Mr Fourex was found in a ditch beside a suburban Brisbane road a day later. Debbie Rasmussen spotted the dirty icon out of the corner of her eye as she drove past.

"We saw what looked like a big white ball and intrigued by what it might be, we stopped the car to have a closer look," Mrs Rasmussen said.

"Once we realised it was Mr Fourex we wrapped him up carefully and took him to the Goodna police station."

Despite not being a big beer drinker, she took the slabs as a reward and handed them out to friends.

In December, 2005, thieves scaled a billboard and cut down a massive 18mx6m poster of Mr Fourex. This time, just 20 slabs were offered for his safe return.

"After all, it is the festive season and 20 cases of beer is a good start, so let's hope they find it in their heart to bring him home," brewery spokesman Mark Powell said.

"We'd love to have him back before Christmas."

There does not appear to be any reports of the man's safe return this time.

Mr Fourex also got "hillbilly hard rock" band Six Foot Hick into a spot of legal bother in 2004, when they put the boater hat-wearing guy's image on a T-shirt but replaced his face with that of former premier Joh Bjelke-Petersen and placed a shotgun in his hand.

Lion Nathan sent a letter that effectively said, "sell any of those shirts and we'll see you in court, sunshine." Singer Geoff Corbett considered fighting it in court, but couldn't afford the legal fees.

"I guess they're protecting their trademark, but they obviously can't take a bloody joke," Corbett said. "We weren't having a go at XXXX, or Joh, for that matter. They're icons. We reckon they're public property."

Bonus XXXX fact: Keith Dunstan's *The Amber Nectar* includes a story about the Australian Trade Commission trying to promote the beer in France. They were hamstrung by the fact that Fourex was also the name of a famous French condom. Which meant the beer's famous slogan "I can feel a Fourex coming on" took on a rather different meaning.

EIGHTEEN
THE DARWIN STUBBY

In the homes of the 1960s and 1970s, no self-respecting pool room would have been complete without a Darwin Stubby on a bar or shelf. It could be left full, but an empty bottle carried more kudos. The implication it carried was that you were such a tops bloke that you may well have necked all of the two litres of beer contained within. And then perhaps had a nice, long nap.

It was also a sign that you'd actually travelled to the Northern Territory as the great big fat bottles weren't all that easy to come by anywhere else in the country.

Right now, they're not easy to come by in the Northern Territory either, with Carlton and United Breweries deciding there weren't enough pool rooms still needing a Darwin Stubby to make it worthwhile to keep producing them. Okay, that wasn't their stated reason, but the underlying truth is there – the Darwin Stubby was a pool room decoration, not something you'd pick up on a Friday night to drink while watching the footy …

The Northern Territory has a reputation for being, well, a little bit different to the rest of the country. Whether it's the heat, the long miles of empty red dirt between one place and the next, the crocodiles, the "wild frontier" attitude of some residents or the fact that it just seems so far away from the rest of the country, it's a place that is almost a law unto itself.

If any place in the country was going to be touted as the home of a bloody great big bottle of beer, it would be the Northern Territory and its capital of Darwin. The two-litre bottle of beer known as the Darwin Stubby just wouldn't make sense if it was, say the Sydney Stubby or the Melbourne Stubby – though if those both existed you know the two cities' rivalry would lead to an endless contest of "our bottle's bigger than yours". But the Darwin Stubby just works – and no other state is game to compete with them when it comes to size.

So it's curious that it wasn't a Darwinian who invented it. The big bottle actually came from the CUB headquarters in Melbourne and had more to do with economics than any preconceived ideas of what the Northern Territory was like, or how thirsty the populace was.

Before there could be a Darwin Stubby there had to be a brewery making beer to fill it, because even if purchasers like to show off the empty bottle in their pool rooms, they don't want to buy them in that condition. The brewery up north didn't happen until 1957, when CUB beat Perth's Swan Brewery in a race to set one up in Darwin. Prior to that all of Darwin's beers came from, first, CUB in Melbourne and, after 1939, from Perth, when the government rationed beer and CUB decided it made more sense to deliver it from the Western Australian capital rather than Melbourne.

In October 1957, CUB opened the first Darwin brewery in the suburb of Winnellie. Less than a year later, the number-crunchers at CUB in Melbourne reckoned it was too expensive to keep sending empty 750ml bottles up to Darwin, go through the cost of filling them and then trying to get the empties returned. So they came up with the idea of combining three longnecks into one bottle – a 2.25-litre bottle. They went for another first, adding a deposit fee into the price as an inducement to get people to return the empties. Hindsight would prove that the expectation that people would return these bottles was severely misguided; they were unique and went onto become a collector's item and souvenirs for tourists.

While the big bottles are known for carrying NT Draught – so much so that "Darwin Stubby" and "NT Draught" are often used interchangeably when people write about the Top End beer – those first bottles were filled with Victoria Bitter. Also, for the first decade of their existence they were known as the Carlton VB Half Gallon bottle – it wouldn't be until the introduction of the throwdown-style of beer bottle known as the stubby, that the name Darwin Stubby would come into being.

As for NT Draught making its way into the bottles, that didn't happen until 1973 with the merger of CUB and Swan in Darwin, which formed the NT Brewery. After that time, NT Draught finally made its way in the Darwin Stubby and on the label.

People being what they are, it was only a matter of time before a pub in Darwin started a Darwin Stubby drinking contest. According to Douglas R Barrie's history of the bottle it was the Koala Hotel which started just such a contest. In 1979, the *NT News* reported that Victorian carpenter Max Van Dennesse knocked one back in 62.34 seconds. Barrie's book claims the Guinness world record for drinking a Darwin Stubby to be 62 seconds – a record that will never be beaten after CUB reduced the volume of the Darwin Stubby from 2.25-litres to two litres in 1983.

But the contests continued until the early 1990s when the liquor laws insisted alcohol could only be served in standard measures and efforts to encourage excessive drinking were frowned upon.

In 1989, the Darwin Stubby started a nomadic life. That year CUB shut up shop in Darwin and moved the Stubby operations over to Cairns in Queensland. This meant a beer named NT Draught wasn't being brewed in the Northern Territory nor was a bottle named the Darwin Stubby being filled in Darwin. A year later it moved again, to Brisbane and, again in 1992, to Yatala, Queensland. It wasn't until 1996 that CUB built a new brewery in the Northern Territory and sent the Darwin Stubby back across the border.

Five years later it was on the road again, heading back to Yatala when CUB closed the Northern Territory brewery. In 2005, the bottling machinery was sent to the Matilda Bay Garage Brewery in Dandenong, Victoria. Three years later, it would be pumping out 24,000 Darwin Stubbies a year.

The big bottle celebrated its 50th in 2008 but, despite those big numbers at the Matilda Bay Garage Brewery, the Darwin Stubby's days were drawing to a close. In 2015 the march of consolidation and cost savings finally caught up with the Darwin Stubby. CUB decided it would cut back on production, with an apparent view to discontinuing it altogether.

"At over two litres, it was certainly the biggest beer in Australia, if not the world," a CUB spokesman said.

"In recent times however, it's become a product people pick up as an item of interest or souvenir rather than being a beer made for general consumption. We've looked at many options to keep the Darwin Stubby alive on a full-time basis, however due to decreasing volumes and increasing costs associated with such a special, niche product, continuing to brew it on a regular basis just didn't add up."

While the bloody great bottle of beer was sent to the great recycling bin in the sky, CUB still had plans to keep the beer NT Draught going. But just not on a full-time basis – instead it would likely be added to CUB's run of heritage beers, to be trotted out on tap every now and then.

The Slab

Easter Egg #3

Getting drunk before you're about to start a big job is almost never a good idea. But for two men who signed up to join the ill-fated expedition of Robert Burke and William Wills, getting smashed was a very good idea - maybe even a lifesaver.

Burke and Wills got it into their heads to cross the continent from Melbourne in the south to the Gulf of Carpentaria in the north. To say they didn't fully understand what they were doing seems an understatement; among the equipment they chose to bring along were extremely unessential items like a cedar-topped oak table with matching chairs, 12 dandruff brushes and a Chinese gong.

The expedition was due to leave Melbourne on August 20, 1860, but Henry Creber got the sack the night before. Another member of the expedition party, George Landells, accused Creber of drunkenness and dobbed him into the petulant Burke, who punted him. Burke also gave the flick to expedition member Robert Fletcher for supporting his mate Creber.

On August 20, there was a big celebration in Royal Park, Melbourne, where 15,000 spectators gathered to see off the 20-strong expedition party. Yet, before it left the number dropped by one, thanks to a sly grog shop operating behind the camel stables. Expedition member and former policeman Owen Cohen found the sly grog store and overindulged, becoming "a little too hilarious through excess of beer". Burke, who was fast establishing himself as a bit of a dick, sacked Cohen on the spot.

The expedition hadn't even started and it was already three men down. More would quit during the walk; Landells resigned and walked home after Burke the Dick decided to dump the rum Landells had brought for the camels in the belief it prevented scurvy. Charles Ferguson was sacked a month into the walk and challenged Burke to a duel and a number of others were discharged along the way.

Which was good news for them - it meant they avoided being among the seven men who died on the expedition. Yes, Burke and Wills were among the dead.

Bonus Burke fact: As well as being a dick, Burke was a really creepy man. In 1854, when he was 30 years old he became infatuated with a 15-year-old actress named Julia Mathews. He even followed her on tour, which we call "stalking" today. His obsession didn't fade either; it has been suggested that Burke was hoping to impress Mathews by going on the expedition. He was also hoping to marry her and asked for her hand just before leaving. She wisely said no, but Burke still made her sole beneficiary in his will - which he changed while on the trek to give it all to his sister.

NINETEEN
BREATHE EASY WITH RBT

Some of the effects of random breath testing – at least in NSW – are obvious. For example, there are people who are alive today because of it. People who didn't die in a car crash because they choose not to try and drive while over the limit. And the innocent driver and passengers in the other car they would have hit – they got to stay alive too.

Yep, a strong random breath testing regime in NSW saved a lot of people. But it also did a whole lot of other things as well. It effectively created a whole new market segment for brewers in low-alcohol beer. And it gave people a socially acceptable way to cut down on their drinking and refuse that beer while saving face at the same time - "sorry mate, I can't have another beer. Want to make sure I'm under the limit".

Those changes have all been for the better. So it's surprising to realise there was such strong resistance to the introduction of RBT - just about everyone from the pubs to politicians to civil liberty groups hated the very idea …

Once upon a time, it was pretty much okay to drink and drive in Australia. Seriously. Yeah, technically it *was* illegal - but you could drink so much beer that people could see it floating behind your eyes like a spirit level and then get behind the wheel of your car. As long as you could get home without running into anyone or anything – or causing a police officer in a passing patrol car to think you were drunk – you were sweet.

No, I'm not making this up. Police were no great fans of drinking and driving and would regularly issue warnings like this one Sergeant Adams of the Wollongong Police Traffic Command gave via the *Illawarra Mercury* in 1950.

"Just a small quantity of intoxicating liquor might upset the mental balance of some drivers and cause them to do something or fail to do something that eventually ends up in an accident. That accident may result in the death of your wife or child or some other disinterested person who may be in the path of your crazy car, out of control, driven by a man who put his own selfish desire first – a man who must have his few beers."

The police could test you to see if you'd been drinking alcohol. And there were blood-alcohol limits set in legislation – in the 1960s Western Australia had the now-frankly ridiculous mark of 0.15, which would see you three times over the limit today. They would soon drop it in line with the other states to 0.08 and then 0.05. But here's the thing – that test would usually only happen after an accident or driving offence. Which effectively meant that driving with a skinful wasn't a crime, it was what you did while driving drunk that got you in trouble. It was a law that told drivers, "hey, are you tanked? Well, roll the dice and drive anyway. You might get lucky and make it home safely". And people did that – loads of people. Because everyone thought they were fine behind the wheel after a few drinks.

That all started to change in December 1982, when NSW introduced random breath testing. It wasn't the first state to introduce it; Victoria brought in random breath testing in July 1976 but it is telling that no state followed its lead for six years. That's because the Victorian effort wasn't whole-hearted; they had short-term blitzes which had a similar short-term impact on crash statistics. What NSW – and Tasmania, who brought in RBT just a month later in January 1983 – did was what academic Ross Homel has called the "boots and all" approach. They launched it with a huge amount of publicity, made sure the RBT units were visible on the streets and went hard with enforcement – in that first year 923,272 tests were conducted, a figure that equates to one in three drivers in NSW. To spell out the different approaches of NSW and Victoria – in the first year of testing, Victoria carried out just 19,006 tests.

Today random breath testing is an accepted part of law enforcement; we recognise the need for it and no one has a problem with the police doing it. Back in the early 1980s when Labor MP George Paciullo wanted it brought in the idea of random breath testing was highly controversial. The road toll at that time was staggering – in 1981, a year before random breath testing was introduced, 1291 people died on the state's roads. That's a shocking figure from today's perspective but it wasn't enough for many motorists to accept that something had to change.

But Paciullo knew something had to be done. As chairman of the inaugural Staysafe Committee – a body charged with tackling the road toll – he was in the right place to do something. But he really had his work cut out for him, because there was a whole lot of opposition to his plan, some of it from surprising quarters.

One not-at-all surprising opponent was the alcohol industry, who claimed it would spell doom and gloom for pubs across the state. The then NSW Australian Hotels Association president Barry McInerney, incredibly, saw it as unfair to target drink drivers. "The apparent inaction by authorities in combating the dangerous non-drinking driver," he said, "is an unfair attack on responsible, sane drinking drivers who pose absolutely no danger on the road." That sort of mentality – that most drivers were totally fine behind the wheel after a night at the pub – was rife.

A Newcastle club actually banned several local ALP members from a function in protest over the idea of RBT. A club spokesman said the limit of "four middies in an hour was an imposition on the working class".

Pollies over the border in Queensland sniggered. Joh Bjelke-Petersen said "it is not a vote-winner" while one of his ministers, Don Lane, went overboard – "Random breath tests are a fascist or Nazi-style approach". (let's play a game - which state was the last in Australia to introduce RBT? If you answered Queensland, you're correct. They brought in RBT legislation in 1988 – six years after it was proven by NSW to be a success).

Even civil liberty groups were opposed to it, because it implied a presumption of guilt over innocence. The idea being that, by pulling someone over for the purposes of a random breath test you were suggesting they were guilty of drink driving, rather than only testing drivers *after* they'd killed someone in an accident. I'm not sure how those groups felt about the civil liberties of those killed by drunk drivers.

Even the Australian Law Reform Commission disliked RBT - "important liberties should not be surrendered on the basis of a hunch or as a consequence of wishful thinking," it said. As you can see, there were a lot of people were on the wrong side of history.

Paciullo even had trouble winning over his own Labor party, with about a third of MPs on his side, a third opposed and a third on the fence when the Labor caucus sat to hear his sales pitch on the idea of an RBT trial.

"When people told me it was politically untenable, I replied that – if we did nothing – we would bear political responsibility for every death and injury caused by drink driving from then on," Paciullo remembered.

Of course, the fact that Paciullo had the support of his Premier Neville Wran didn't hurt either (though Wran was dubbed "One can Wran" by some over his support for RBT). Paciullo won the caucus vote, which gave him a three-year trial of RBT from December 1982. And so, on December 17, 1982, the last Friday before Christmas, the testing stations and the booze buses (reconfigured government buses) hit the road.

According to Homel, 200 extra police were recruited for highway patrol work to boost enforcement of RBT and carry out those 923,272 preliminary breath tests in the first year – a massive jump from the 113,985 breath tests conducted in NSW the previous year.

The first years of RBT in NSW had a marked impact on alcohol-related fatalities. According to Homel, during the three years before RBT, the number of drivers and riders with a blood alcohol level over 0.05 was 4.36 a week. In the first four years of RBT, that dropped 36 per cent to 2.81. Total fatal crashes and alcohol-related crashes saw similar declines.

That first year of RBT saw the road toll fall by 300 – irrefutable proof that it worked. Random breath testing would cease to operate on a trial basis and become law in December 1985. By 2001, the road toll would be more than halved compared to that 1291 figure from 1981 – an impressive figure when you take into account the rise in cars on the road in that time.

The success of RBT in NSW sparked the other states into action. "As police in other states saw the effects of what was happening in NSW," Homel told ABC journalist Will Ockenden, "the political opposition just crumbled and they all adopted random breath testing." Victoria and South Australia (which brought it in in October 1981) changed their approach to be more in line with the NSW regime. Western Australia and finally Queensland would eventually come to the party in 1988 with their own RBT laws. Queensland was the last state to do it, and some suggest it came into force as a means for the new National party government to distance itself from the systemic corruption that was being uncovered by the Fitzgerald inquiry.

RBT also changed our drinking habits. It opened up a new market segment for the brewing industry – light beer. It also led to the creation of non-alcoholic beers, which didn't really take off. After RBT, people began to use it as an excuse to say no to a beer in a group situation – at least in NSW. According to one study, in 1989 only 48 per cent of NSW people said they'd never used the excuse of police breath testing to reduce their drinking. This compared to 57 per cent in Queensland, 63 per cent in Victoria and 67 per cent in Western Australia.

Homel said RBT also had an effect on beer drinking in pubs in NSW, which declined for a period relative to other states. "However, the most marked effects appear to have been a trend away from on-premise drinking, especially draught beer, to buying packaged alcohol and consuming it away from licensed premises," Homel wrote.

He also suggests that an adverse consequence of RBT and the encouragement to leave the car at home may be an increase in drunkenness and violence on trains as well as in the vicinity of pubs at closing time.

But there is no doubt that people are alive today due to RBT. In NSW police have estimated it has saved more than 7000 lives since it was introduced in 1982. If you're one of those people, or in their family, you'd certainly see RBT as undeniably a good thing.

The Slab

TWENTY
DRINKING FOR AUSTRALIA

Just about everything about a modern athlete is under scrutiny these days. Their bodies are checked to ensure there are no injuries present that will limit their ability to perform. Their fitness is tracked, through everything from beep tests to heart-rate monitors. They get given nutrition advice and diets to follow to make sure the sporting machine that is their body is getting appropriate fuels.

In some sports even the athlete's private life is under scrutiny. They go out to a pub or club you can bet your life there's some dickhead looking to take some incriminating footage on his phone so he can make a quick buck selling it to the media.

These factors all conspire to make it highly unlikely that we will ever again see the likes of David Boon's alleged feat while in the air between Australia and England. Which isn't entirely a bad thing. There can't be too many people who would like to share a flight from Australia to England with drunken cricketers ...

The Slab

It was a big year, 1977. *Star Wars* opened in the cinemas. The Sex Pistols released their debut album. And some cricketers decided to booze on while flying to England.

And I mean, really booze on.

That was the year Doug Walters effectively created the unofficial sport of "drinking as much as you bloody can before the plane's wheels kiss the tarmac." Inklings of the idea arose on a 1973 flight back from the Caribbean when Walters and moustachioed keeper Rodney Marsh went at it.

But it really grew into its own in 1977, once the stewardesses closed the cabin doors and started serving booze. While it seems most of the team was involved in the competition and bets were placed, according to spin bowler Kerry O'Keeffe, Walters and Marsh started out as the favourites, with the drinking tally written on a sick-bag. As it turned out, they were the last men standing – or maybe swaying – as the plane neared Heathrow.

"The leaders, Walters and Marsh, will definitely fight it out to the finish," O'Keeffe wrote in his book *According to Skull*.

"They look shabby. Marsh has fallen asleep and there is saliva making its way down his chin. Walters is attempting to light the filter of his 60th cigarette for the journey."

When the plane landed, they checked the tally which was kept on the back of that sick-bag. The winner was Walters with 44 cans, ahead of Marsh by one tinnie. Though Marsh would maintain he matched his team-mate can for can.

Such a narrow defeat must have rankled the bristle-lipped cricketer because he had a crack at the title on a 1983 flight to the mother country. Dennis Lillee tried to discourage his mate, lest he end up watching the World Cup from a bed "in the drying-out ward of some London hospital". He did this by the counter-intuitive approach of trying to get him drunk before they met up with the flight in Sydney.

It didn't work – Marsh made it all the way to 45 cans. But it was a close-run thing.

"I swear to this day I could see beer about to spill over his bottom teeth onto the floor," Lillee recalls of Marsh's 43rd beer.

Then he whispered he was done while sipping on the record-tying 44th can. But there was no turning back - his team-mates effectively force-fed his 45th beer and loaded him on a trolley to wheel him through customs.

That mark stood for just six years before a stout Tasmanian named Boon and his big moustache boarded a plane headed to England and The Ashes. While the man himself steadfastly refuses to talk about the events on that plane, the fact that he also doesn't seem to want to refute them speaks volumes about the veracity of the story.

And so does the testimony of some of his team-mates on the plane. In a fascinating article by journalist Peter Lalor, Geoff Lawson, Dean Jones and Moustache Mate Merv Hughes spilled the beans on Boon's herculean 52-can effort.

Lawson told Lalor he was the scorekeeper - again keeping tally on a sick-bag. But there was no competition this time.

"Nobody accompanied Boony," Lawson said. "We were all a bit more sensible. There weren't too many big drinkers in the team then. I think the culture of the '70s changed through the '80s."

But it appears Boony didn't need anyone to compete against, he was happy being the only man in the race. And the man obviously knew how to pace himself. Near the end of the flight, coach Bob Simpson reportedly woke up to cheers and heard the pilot announcing Boony had sunk his 52nd can.

"Simpson went purple with anger and I mentioned to (selector Laurie) Sawle that maybe Boony should be sent home and I would bat in his spot," Jones recalled.

For the record, it was suggested at one stage that Boon drained 56 cans. But it seems 52 is now the agreed-upon figure. Though we'll never hear that from the mouth of Boon himself.

Boon walked off the plane unaided and, soon thereafter, Simpson called a team meeting and told them no one should speak a word of this. But that horse had well and truly bolted – Hughes put his hand up and admitted that he'd already talked about it during a radio interview.

Years later Simpson himself confirmed the drinking record happened, in a video interview on YouTube.

"We had David Boon break the world record to England for the number of cans drunk," Simpson said. "David walked off the plane and attended the press conference. He was spoken to and never looked like doing anything as silly again."

Taking away the larrikin, blokey aspect of it, 52 cans in 24 hours *is* a pretty silly thing to do. A can holds 375ml of beer, which means Boon drank 19.5 litres of beer. That's roughly two-thirds of a keg. Jeez, drinking that much *water* would be enough of a struggle.

Funny how times change. Boony is now a bit of a legend for drinking all those cans and a segment of the Australian population love him for it. But were a cricketer – or a rugby league or AFL player – to do it today, they would have scorn rained down on them from such a great height.

Incidentally, Walters refutes Boony's right to hold the title of King of "drinking as much as you bloody can before the plane's wheels kiss the tarmac". That's because Walters reckons the scorekeeper fiddled with the stats by counting the beers Boon drank in the departure lounge. For Walters, only the beers drunk while inside the plane count.

While many figured Boon's record would stand for all time, some have put forward Hall of Fame baseballer Wade Boggs' claimed effort of 107 beers in 24 hours on one particular liquid day back in 2005. In the spirit of the game, I think it's about more than just a straightforward totalling of beers drunk. If someone drank 60 cans of light beer on the flight from Australia to England, that wouldn't be the same as Boon's effort, now would it?

There are a few things which make Boggs' challenge shaky. First-up, he was necking Miller Lite, which has 4.2 per cent, while Boon did his thing with the strong Victoria Bitter which weighed in at 4.9 per cent.

Secondly, Walters' claim of departure lounge drinking aside, Boony did all his work in a plane. At altitude most of the time, and the effects of alcohol are greater at altitude. The majority of Boggs' boozing took place on the ground. While Boggs did take a cross-country US flight on the day in question, that was only seven hours in a plane, which means he had 17 hours of drinking on the ground. And he started his beer count before he got to the airport, then at the airport, during a stopover and at a party after he landed.

So I think you'll agree, Boggs' effort doesn't stack up against Boon's record. Furthermore, I have my doubt about whether Boggs' effort even happened – if you drank that much beer how the hell could you keep track of the number of cans? He'd have enough trouble trying to remember his own name.

TWENTY-ONE
ALAN BOND: HOW TO LOSE MONEY AND ALIENATE DRINKERS

If nicknames are any indication, some Australians had a soft spot for failed millionaire tycoon Alan Bond. They did the Aussie thing of whacking a Y at the end of his name, thus transforming him to Bondy. Christopher Skase was another failed millionaire who was doing the rounds at the same time as Bond but no one ever called him Skasey.

But despite being granted the honour of a Y at the end of his name, Bondy did his level best to ensure he trashed his own reputation and gave people a reason to hate him. Some hated him because he left debts of more than $1 billion and was found guilty of stealing at least that much from one of his companies.

Others hated him because he mucked around with their beer, or tried to take away their hotels after they'd sunk their savings in them. And this was after Bondy had bought their breweries because they were cranking out dollars …

These days, it's getting trickier for the big breweries to make a buck. Sure, they're not exactly standing in the breadline wearing rags or seen at intersections with a squeegee and a bucket of water but, with the steady rise of craft beer, the big guys are seeing their sales going ever so slowly downhill.

It wasn't always this way. Go back in time a little and owning a brewery was a licence to print money. And also a licence to pretty much sit back and do bugger-all and watch as that cash just flowed through the door. Each state had its own beer and you'd be unlikely to see, say VB, make its way north of the Victorian border or Resch's end up for sale in Queensland. This was partially why it was so stupidly easy to make money out of a brewery. People were loyal to their state drop. They supported their beer like they would a footy team and were happy to pay to continue to support it. Their beer was the elixir of the Gods and the stuff others drank over the border was dog piss. Even though most punters had no chance in hell of picking their beer in a blind taste test with those from other states.

If you were the owner of one of these big breweries, you effectively had a whole state to yourself, with limited competition and a rusted-on group of consumers who would drink your beer from their teenage years right through to when they karked it. Keep a very light hand on the tiller and everything would be fine, the money would keep rolling in. Honestly, it seemed such a guaranteed easy way to make money that a man would have to work really hard to screw things up.

That man was Alan Bond. He managed to screw things up in two different states (and, as an aside, two different countries as well). In one state, he managed to alienate those rusted-on drinkers who had bought his beer for ages. Not only that, his actions also created a competitor for those disheartened drinkers to flock to in droves. In the other state, he drove the pub owners who were selling his products into the arms of a rival brewer, and gave his own beers a very big black eye in terms of public perception.

And these were the actions of a man who bought the breweries because they were *making* money. A man who needed the money the breweries were raking in to fund some of his other investments. His inept handling of the breweries was what, in large part, led to Bond's rather spectacular downfall.

The Western Australian big spender had already borrowed heavily to buy Swan Brewery in 1982 and it seems he didn't run that into the ground. Though he also didn't seem to work out that whatever he was doing with Swan was working so he should try and do it again when he bought some other breweries.

His troubles started when he made an audacious purchase of Castlemaine Tooheys in 1985. And by audacious I mean the biggest corporate takeover the country had seen – according to journalist Paul Barry's book *The Rise and Fall of Alan Bond* it cost Bond Corporation $1200 billion. That's roughly four times what the empire was worth at the time. No matter how much you love beer, in my book that's overspending.

That deal gave him the leading beer brand in Queensland - XXXX – and an almost dominant share of the NSW market through Tooheys. Add to that the virtual monopoly he had in Western Australia with Swan and Bondy owned almost half of the Australian beer market. *Half* the market. If he played his cards right, he'd be swimming in money. But, of course, he played his cards very badly. In less than five years it all went to hell in a handbasket.

In just 18 months after taking over, Bond and his team pissed off the parochial Queensland drinking population by ripping down the old Castlemaine sign from the brewery in the Brisbane suburb of Milton and replacing it with a Bond Brewing sign. Then he redesigned the XXXX cans as well, so that "Bond Brewing" and the address of its Western Australian HQ appeared instead of the Milton address. To a Queensland drinker who saw XXXX as part of their state's identity, it seemed as though "their" beer had been taken away from them.

That wasn't enough for the Bond team. They had more things they needed to do to ensure everything was royally screwed up. Just before Christmas the brewery's hotel owners saw their free credit period cut from 30 days to just seven. "It nearly sent a lot of people to the wall, including me," said Bond's soon-to-be nemesis Bernie Power to Paul Barry. "We had done business with that company for 50-odd years, and they did it without as much as a phone call or a letter."

While all the publicans were angry at Bond, Power was so furious he took the bold step of starting up his own brewery.

"It became quite clear to me that there was a lot of discontent in the marketplace," he told beer journalist Matt Kirkegaard. "Hoteliers and others were angry, frustrated and didn't like the company. It was quite clear to me as a hotelier that there would be an opportunity to build a brewery."

So Bond's actions created not only a rival but a whole lot of customers for that rival. Still, it took a bit of effort to convince the banks he was serious, but Power got his brewery up and running. Power's Bitter quickly snaffled 10 per cent of the Queensland market. But, as he told Kirkegaard, he was playing catch-up from the start.

"The facts are, we ran out of beer, literally, from the first day, and never caught up. What we should have done was focused on our state so we could supply it properly and manage it properly."

He ended up partnering with Bond rival Carlton and United, ultimately selling out in 1992. By which time he'd outlasted Bond by a good two years.

At the same time as he was mucking things up in Queensland, the Bond team was also wrecking things in NSW. In that state, he had the leading brand – Tooheys. It was making plenty of cash, but it wasn't enough for Bond. Looking to squeeze an extra $30 million profit out of the brewer, Bond Brewing decided to throw 130 Tooheys leaseholders out of their pubs – giving them 30 days to get out and offering no compensation for the goodwill they'd built up. Technically, Bond was within his rights to do this – the lease agreements allowed Tooheys to repossess the pubs. But the old bosses had assured the tenants that would never happen, that Tooheys had never in its history evicted someone and they'd even encouraged tenants to pump money into improving their pubs.

And now, the big guy wanted to kick the little guy out on the street. The tenants weren't rich by any means - many had sunk all their money into the pubs in the belief they'd be able to sell at a profit at some time in the future. The stress was so much for one tenant that he rented a hotel room, put a plastic bag over his head and suffocated himself.

In order to fight for their financial lives, the Tooheys tenants formed an action group. At one stage their envoys were told by Bond's people the tycoon's message was "burn the bastards". The members of the action group pitched in to create a fighting fund to take the matter to court, while the old guard at Tooheys kept trying to convince the new boss how much damage he was doing to the company's brand. And he was – you can bet your life none of these tenants kept selling Tooheys during this whole process. They started buying kegs from rival breweries like Reschs and Foster's, chipping away at Tooheys' market share.

The case went to court, and both sides could claim a win – and by this time the Bond camp needed to claim some sort of win in the brewing world. Bond could still turf them into the street when the leases expired, but the tenants would get compensated for the money they'd invested in the pub. In the process of the two sides negotiating what level of compensation would be appropriate, Bondy had another go at wrecking the company he bought for the money it generated. He issued another 13 tenants with notices to quit so Bond Brewing could take over the pubs. Those tenants received compensation offers below market value – Barry reported that one Newcastle tenant was offered $350,000 for the lease he had bought two years earlier for $395,000 and which brokers had valued at $700,000.

The farce dragged on until 1989, when Bond had to give up – Bond Brewing was so short of cash it could no longer afford to buy the tenants out. Despite Bond's best efforts, Bond Brewing was still in the black – it was the only part of his empire making any money. But it was way, way, waaayy short of what he needed to prop up the rest of his fading empire.

Still Bond had done serious damage to the Castlemaine-Tooheys market share. When he launched the takeover, it had a 45 per cent share of the Australian beer market. When Lion bought it in September 1990, it had dropped to 37 per cent (Lion also picked up Swan Brewery in the deal). Tooheys, in particular was hit hard, falling from a 60 per cent market share in 1985 to 40 per cent just five years later.

Bond's time at the helm at Toohey's had a small positive moment. According to J Peter Thoeming's history of the brewer, in 1986 – during Bondy's time – it was the first in Australia to introduce beer cans with a non-detachable opening, which replaced the old ring-pull tab that separated from the can after opening and whose sharp edges would result in an untold number of foot lacerations when discarded on the ground.

As an aside, Bond also managed to lose money on beer in the United States. In 1987, he bought the G Heileman Brewing Company. That too lost market share and ended up so overloaded with debt that it filed for bankruptcy protection in 1990. In the end, it was offloaded to rival brewer Stroh for less than 25 per cent of what Bondy bought it for.

The Slab

TWENTY-TWO
THE FAMILY FIGHTS BACK

Australians love an underdog. Put a little guy up against a big guy and we'll throw our support behind the little guy. Even if we think the little guy has no chance, we'll still cheer for them, because jeez, we'd like them to smash the big guy.

In 2005 it seemed like that little guy had no chance. That was when Australian brewing behemoth Lion made a hostile play for Coopers, a brewery where many of the shareholders have the same name as the label on the beer. Indeed, some of those with the surname of Cooper were actually running the company that Thomas Cooper kicked off way back in 1862.

Now, when a family-owned company who makes beer is looking to fight off an unwelcome takeover by a giant in the industry, Australians were sure to gravitate to Coopers.

Even if we thought the little guy didn't have a snowball's chance in hell against that big brewer with all its money and lawyers …

It was an argument over a beer bottle that laid the foundations for the biggest stoush between two brewers in recent memory. In 2005 Lion launched a hostile takeover of South Australia's family-owned brewer Coopers. But 15 years earlier Lion had intervened to settle a dispute over that beer bottle and help out Coopers.

The beer bottle dispute started in the 1990s. Coopers was one of three brewers that owned the Adelaide Bottle Company – along with small set-up Oakbank and the CUB-owned SA Brewing. The bottle company had been supplying all three with refillable beer bottles under an agreement that dated back to 1929. That agreement meant Coopers would get the same bottles as SA Brewing. The latter launched a new beer – Eagle Blue – and got a new mid-neck bottle called the Stubby Mark II.

"We said we also wanted the Stubby Mark II," Coopers MD Tim Cooper told the Sunday Mail in 2005, "but SA Brewing refused to give us access."

With no other option, Coopers launched legal action which slowly wound its way through the courts. In 1993, Lion bought SA Brewing and the company appointed Wayne Jackson as the managing director, which meant he inherited the Stubby Mark II dispute. And he realised it was in Lion's best interests to solve the dispute. Big brewing rival CUB had been eyeing off the South Australian market and the bottle dispute was a bit of a festering sore between Coopers and Lion. Jackson's concern was, should Coopers look to sell or enter in a joint venture, it would likely be with CUB rather than Lion. So from Jackson's point of view, putting the whole Stubby Mark II argument to bed may well block CUB from forcing its way into the South Australian market.

At the same time, Coopers was worried about Lion's intentions. SA Brewing had owned a 26 per cent shareholding in Coopers at the time Lion bought the business. When Lion made a move to acquire those shares, that put the wind up the Cooper family, figuring the bigger brewer might be up to something.

To appease everyone at Coopers and ward off any possible merger with CUB, Jackson made the deal that saw those shares go back to Coopers, with the proviso that Lion could buy any shares not wanted by existing shareholders or the Coopers superannuation fund AMP.

In return, Coopers had to drop all litigation, including that which revolved around the stubby bottle. To make things even clearer, Jackson gave a personal pledge that Lion "has no wish, intention or aspiration, etc, to own or control or exert management influence over Coopers".

And so everything was fine and dandy. At least until 1998 when megabrewer Kirin snaffled up a 45 per cent stake in Lion. Figuring megabrewers are always hungry and worried they might be next on the menu, the Coopers board took action. They had their suits tell those suits over at Lion that the share deal was no more because control of the bigger company had substantially changed. Lion's lawyers responded with a "nah-uh. No way". But with a lot more legal jargon involved.

Coopers started legal action in 2002 to declare the share deal invalid. Lion, on the other hand, kept trying to smooth things over. Which lasted until the Coopers board rejected a joint venture pitch in 2003. Then the Lion board said, "bugger this for a game of soldiers" and launched a hostile takeover, offering $260 a share – which would later be raised to $310 a share.

From there it was effectively a race – Lion was trying to get enough shares to take control while Coopers looked to change the constitution to scratch out the share deal from the company constitution. Coopers got part of the way there on September 2, 2005 – the day after the takeover was launched – when the courts declared the deal invalid.

It cleared the way for a shareholder meeting to change the constitution in December. It was what you could call a shellacking for Lion – a massive 93.42 per cent of shareholders voted in favour of constitutional changes that would make it impossible for the big brewer to buy shares. The change also appears to make it impossible for *any* brewer to own Coopers shares, which effectively makes the company takeover-proof.

In hindsight the vote was a foregone conclusion. Coopers really is a family-owned company – around 90 per cent of shareholders are linked to founder Thomas Cooper by birth or marriage. Part of the share structure reportedly includes "A" shares, which are completely owned by those who trace their ancestry to Cooper's first wife Anne, while the "B" shares are owned solely by those descended from his second wife Sarah.

For these people, Coopers shares are about more than just the money. As Lion found out.

TWENTY-THREE
AN ARMY OF TALKING BOONY DOLLS

Yep, it's another chapter that features David Boon. If we count the introduction that's three appearances in this book - probably Boony's first hat-trick.

More recently, the man with the moustache turned his back on beer to flog Canadian Club. But for mine, I prefer to remember him for his services to beer. For he was once beer's best friend. And not just because of all those cans he allegedly knocked back on a flight from Australia to England – though that certainly doesn't hurt.

Boony was also the face of Victoria Bitter for a few years in the early 2000s. He let them poke fun at his belly and then signed on to see thousands of Baby Boonys created as part of a genius marketing campaign that gave VB a shot in the arm in terms of sales.

Even if the company ended up regretting that those dolls glorified binge-drinking. Maybe they should have asked Boony to drink responsibly ...

Say you were an Australian beer company and you wanted to make a miniature talking version of an Australian cricketer. I don't know why you would have wanted to do that – maybe your product was ailing and you were desperate to give it a shot in the arm.

Anyway, when choosing a cricketer for the aforementioned miniaturisation, Tasmanian David Boon is a sure thing. He's a blokey bloke, he had a bit of a beer gut, he was a character, he had a moustache, you could put a Y at the end of his name without it sounding stupid and he allegedly drank all those beers on a flight from Australia to England. So we knew he liked a beer. Or 52 – *allegedly*.

The idea to mini-me Boony came from the marketing types at George Patterson Y&R advertising agency. When they started fishing around for a cricketer to miniaturise, no one else was in with a chance – the job was always going to be Boon's to refuse. Well, in hindsight, that seems like a no brainer, but David Boon wasn't actually the first choice. Before the Boony brainwave, they were going to offer a talking bat or a talking ball. Yeah, they sound like dumb ideas to me too.

So in the summer of 2005 the guys at Y&R forgot about talking bats and balls, wised up and looked to Boony (who probably knew the value of the idea – he has a degree in marketing from Charles Sturt University) to help CUB and parent company Foster's lift the flagging fortunes of VB, which had been selling fewer cartons than they would like. Tagged "Boonanza", the promotional campaign saw the creation of a little David Boon doll dressed in the green and gold of the Australian One-Day side.

The idea can be traced all the way back to Voltron – yes, that giant robot made up of four metallic lions. In the 1990s, the creator of the Voltron franchise looked at ways to inject some life into the franchise (aka "make more money"). He came up with a way to use technology to get the toys to interact with the show when it was on TV. The same technology had also been used in an interactive Batmobile that talked along with the Batman TV series.

A Y&R director had been in the US in 2004 and found out about the technology and the company figured it was a way to leverage VB's sponsorship of the cricket that summer. "We thought perhaps we could do a talking cricket ball," George Patterson Y&R promotions manager Iain Crittenden told *The Age* journalist Malcolm Maiden.

Though that talking cricket ball idea was obviously ditched when Boony was on board. There were two ways to get yourself one of the 200,000 Talking Boonys that first year. You could purchase a case of VB and text your details and a unique code on the cartoon and they'd charge you $5 and send you one. Alternatively, at some bottle shops you could buy two cartons and have your mini Boony handed to you there and then.

Inside the Boony doll was a 60-second sound chip that included more than 35 unique phrases. With the help of an internal timer set to eastern standard time, he'd "activate" an hour before the cricket started, his first words being "get me a VB, the cricket's about to start". Place him near the TV when a one-day cricket match was on that summer and he'd respond to one of four audio triggers broadcast by Channel Nine with some comment about bowling, batting or the falling of a wicket. He could also throw out random phrases that didn't need any audio trigger from the TV – phrases like "anyone seen me thongs?", "Got any nachos – I love nachos" and "I feel like playing Totem Tennis".

This tiny Boony army went live with the first match of the VB One-Day Series on Friday, January 13, 2006. Friday the 13th is normally a day for bad luck, but not for the Talking Boony.

The idea was a huge success for CUB, with the Boony dolls selling out in a few weeks. In the summer of 2005-06, they were so hot they were going for more than $200 each on eBay. They still pop up there from time to time if you missed out back then (but there's no guarantee they still talk). Some newspaper reports claim people were even throwing Boony parties where upwards of 30 of the talking figures would be lined up in front of the TV to form a cricketing chorus.

But, surprisingly, it wasn't actually Boony's voice people were hearing talking back to the TV, Y&R's Crittenden told Maiden. "Boony has a low, gruff voice, and it didn't reproduce," he said. "So we got somebody else to record the lines - with Boony's full blessing."

The whole process of making the Boony dolls wasn't cheap – it would have cost elephant bucks, though CUB marketing manager Cameron MacFarlane declined to put a price on how much they spent on the dolls.

"The units are expensive to produce," MacFarlane said. "You need a brand with serious scale and leverage to pull it off … the scale that we have, our established links to Australian cricket, the sheer volume of VB that is sold - these are things that are not easy to replicate."

The dolls didn't shut up when the cricket was over, either. As late as May 2006 people were reporting their Boony doll was still piping up across the country. "We were surprised to hear such widespread stories of him coming back to life for a second time," Foster's spokeswoman Felicity Watson said. She also warned people not to tinker with Boony's batteries, adding that "people can rest assured, he can't talk forever".

That he would make a return the following summer was a no brainer once the sales figures came in. That Summer of Boony saw VB have its best sales in a decade. And it won an award for Y&R at the Cannes Advertising Festival – the Oscars for advertisers.

The following summer, he brought a friend along with him; another talking doll in the shape of English cricketer Ian Botham. Instead of the one-day series, the pair of dolls – 200,000 of each were made – would focus on the Australia-England Test series. The Botham doll was programmed to chant "Barmy Army ... Barmy Army" and utter phrases like "I love warm beer and lashings of it". There was another change too – to prevent stock "leakage" (ie bottle shop staff stealing the dolls) the Boony and Botham dolls were only available via the web, phone and SMS.

The Botham doll sparked a minor controversy, with a complaint lodged with the Advertising Standards Bureau. In a TV ad to promote the dolls, the Botham doll says "Bugger off, Boony!" – but one irate viewer heard something different. "Botham responds clearly with 'Fuck off, Boony!'. It implies that this kind of language is encouraged and worse, entertaining," the complainant stated.

The bureau dismissed the complaint, stating the ad "did not use the phrase mentioned by the complainant". Perhaps of more concern was another complaint about the ad, which used the phrase "go beer for beer with Boony". "It appears to be promoting a binge drinking session with Boony and mates", said another complainant who was unhappy her eight-year-old kept seeing this high-rotation ad.

A CUB spokesman responded by saying the phrase needed to be viewed in context. "The actual phrase says 'find out how these hairy-lipped legends of the game can go pound for pound, tash for tash, beer for beer right there in your lounge room', he said. "It is indicative of the friendly rivalry between these talking figurines and their namesakes in real life, both today and historically."

The board took this complainant more seriously than the one who head the non-existent "Fuck off, Boony!". "The board agrees that, while the phrase may have glorified drinking beer, it was clearly referring to a beer-drinking incident involving David Boon that was well-known among cricket fans, and it did not of itself encourage unsafe or dangerous practices."

Complaints about swearing and binge drinking aside, that summer the Boonanza campaign was again a success, which prompted a third bite at the cherry. This time Boony was retired and replaced with a doll of the recently retired Shane Warne. The Warnie doll sat in an armchair dressed in an Australian one-day cricket shirt and jeans. His phrases included "Like the Spice Girls, unplayable" and "OK pop in the Warnie highlights tape".

Warne was a questionable choice for a promotional doll. While liked by a segment of cricket fans, Warne lacked the broad appeal of Boon. That may be why the interactive dolls never saw a fourth season – maybe the Warne doll ruined the magic. Or maybe the novelty of the first two years had worn off. One thing's for sure – you can still find Boony dolls on eBay. Tracking down a Warnie doll is quite a bit trickier.

Several years after the dolls had their run, a senior Foster's executive admitted to *Sydney Morning Herald* journalist Chloe Saltau that perhaps that complainant's concerns about binge drinking mentioned a few paragraphs ago had some merit.

"We thought David Boon had a perfect fit with VB," Foster's national marketing director Chris Maxwell told Saltau in 2009. "He was a good Aussie bloke, with good Aussie values. However, we had a lot of criticism around using him in regards to this binge-drinking issue.

"Looking back, we have decided that was the wrong thing to do. We didn't have the foresight to see that this issue was going to be so significant. And in glorifying that behaviour we have added to the issue of the normalisation of binge-drinking in Australia."

Before we end the tale of the Boony dolls, it's worth pointing out that some curious souls ignored the advice of that Foster's spokeswoman Felicity Watson. They tinkered around with his insides and posted their results online. Some worked out how to safely remove and replace his batteries (three AAA batteries) so that he would continue to talk for years. Though he would only be able to say those random phrases that had been programmed into him. And he would say them at random times – like the middle of the night when an odd voice is not really the thing you want to be hearing.

Others actually intentionally killed their Boony with a view to seeing how he worked. This was despite the instructional leaflet warning "Do not unscrew the Talking Boony base. This will cause the unit to malfunction." One such person posted photos of

Boony's guts online (visit mrspeaker.net), which included circuit boards featuring a number of chips. In the process of dismantling Boony, he inadvertently dislodged a wire from the battery terminal, which permanently killed the little guy.

The author also worked out how to pimp the Boony doll in various ways. Google "Reverse Boonjaneering" and you can find out how to amplify the Boony doll, with the help of a soldering iron and a few bits and pieces.

You can also see how to add an LED to see when a "talk window" for Boony opens up, which means you can then play a downloaded wav file of the audible trigger that had been recorded from the TV. This post has drawn hundreds of comments from those other Boony owners keen to work out if they could prolong the talking life of their doll beyond the end of the cricket season. Yes, the Boony figurine sparked the interest of some very curious minds. Funnily enough, there seems much less evidence of anyone wanting to pimp their Warnie doll.

TWENTY-FOUR
WHAT IS AUSTRALIA'S MOST EXPENSIVE BEER?

Different people have different ideas about beer. For the craft beer brigade, it's all about flavour, and the idea of "drink less, drink quality". For the average beer drinker, it's about buying the same slab you've always drunk because, really, all beer tastes the same, right? Besides, who wants to be like one of those wankers in the craft beer brigade.

One particular horror the average drinker has of craft beer is the price. Why, they wonder, would someone pay more than $10 for a schooner when around half that would get you a glass of some other beer. Similarly, why would someone pay $70 or $80 for a case when there are other slabs that cost just $30?

Well, this chapter is going to give them a bit more ammunition. If they thought that was a lot of money to spend on beer, they haven't seen anything yet …

The title-holder of the most expensive beer in Australia, and also one of the most expensive in the world, is Nail Brewing over in Western Australia.

So exactly how much does the world's most expensive beer sell for? How much are we talking? $100? Nope. $200? Nope. $300? Okay, this is going to take forever - Nail's Antarctic Pale Ale was on the market in 2010 for $800. That's more than the previous record-holder, Brew Dog's The End of History, which retailed for $765.

How did Brew Dog justify that price? Well, there's a bit of a gimmick involved – funny that, who'd have thought Brew Dog would have opted for a gimmick. There were only 12 330ml bottles of the beer released (a 55 per cent Belgian ale) and each of those bottles was housed inside taxidermied roadkill. Yes, really. God knows how you were supposed to tell how much beer was left in the bottle.

What about Nail's Antarctic Pale Ale? How did they justify the price? With a gimmick, a very big gimmick. The beer was made with water from an iceberg. From Antarctica. To which they flew by helicopter to carve off the ice. So, yeah, if you're making a beer that uses helicopters and icebergs, then you can start to see why it was so pricey. Also, it was helping out a charity – all the money raised from the sale of the 30 bottles went to anti-whaling group Sea Shepherd.

Nail's brewer John Stallwood also admitted there was a bit of self-promotion about the endeavour.

"I'm always looking at new ideas," he told *The Sydney Morning Herald* in 2010.

"Small breweries have little advertising budget – especially me – so we rely on publicity. Most publicity comes with awards, or if you can think of a good idea."

Perhaps not surprising for a beer that features melted icebergs, Stallwood said every step in the making of the beer featured a challenge to be overcome.

"Probably getting ice from Antarctica was the hardest," he said in perhaps a textbook example of understatement.

"My brother-in-law, Kevin McGinty, and his team flew the helicopter to a giant iceberg and dug a hole. They then melted it down back in Tasmania and brought it to Perth."

The first bottle sold for $800, which gave it the title of most expensive beer in Australia – and possibly the world at that time. "It is great to sell the most expensive bottle of beer in the world but it is all about a good cause," Stallwood said at the time.

"It is also good that a beer about saving the whales is now the most expensive beer in the world rather than high alcohol beer sold in animal carcasses. I think future beers that sell for over $800 won't just be unique but will also be for good causes."

But we didn't have to wait long for a beer to pass the $800 mark, for Antarctic Pale Ale bottle #2 went at auction for a massive $1850. So altogether, those 30 bottles of beer must have earned a nice bit of cash for Sea Shepherd.

But this beer was very much a one-off. When it comes to beers made on a regular basis, what would be the most expensive one in Australia? Well, that crown would have to go to Carlton & United's Crown Ambassador, which was made once a year for a handful of years and tended to retail for $100 for a 750ml bottle. Individually numbered, it came in a fancy bottle which sat inside a red silk-lined box. Yes, they really wanted to make it seem like you were getting your money's worth.

The annual beer was first brewed in 2008. The most infamous vintage was the 2010, which fell victim to an infection from brettanomyces yeast. It was famously detected by beer writer Willie Simpson in what would have to be one of the most uncomfortable beer reviews ever written.

Simpson was sitting down to a meal with CUB's head brewer John Cozens and they'd just enjoyed a bottle of the 2009 vintage.

"The first whiff of the current vintage is rank and confronting," Simpson wrote, "while a quick swallow confirms a certain unwanted presence. I wait for my host's reaction."

Cozens said it contained "a hint of sulphur", which he put down to the hops.

"Beer tasting is highly subjective," Simpson wrote. "Where Cozens detected a whiff of sulphur, I reckon it's chockful with feral yeast flavours and the telltale presence of wet horse blanket. Brettanomyces, to be precise, a wild yeast character known as 'brett', favoured by Belgian lambic beer producers and some English farmhouse cider-makers, but feared by most winemakers and brewers alike."

Simpson surmised the brett infection came from the oak barrels the beer had been aged in and which had previously held white wine. CUB did some lab testing and confirmed to the *Crikey* website that brett was there.

"It wasn't our intention for brett to feature in the 2010 vintage but we're still incredibly pleased with the end result," Cozens told *Crikey*.

"We can't 100 per cent pinpoint the source of the brett given some time has passed since we brewed the beer."

Still, the presence of an infection – albeit one that is an asset for some beers - wasn't really a good look for a beer that tagged itself as high-quality. It was something Crown Ambassador hasn't been able to shake off either – around the time of the beer's annual release someone would always bring up the troubled 2010 vintage.

The Slab

Easter Egg #4

Brewers can talk about their beer having body. In the case of one Sydney brewery, that phrase took on a very different meaning. As in actual dead bodies finding their way into the beer – or at least tiny bits thereof. The brewery in question was Albion Brewery, started in 1827 by former convict Samuel Terry. It was located in Elizabeth Street because it was close to fresh water that flowed down to Darling Harbour.

The brewery itself no longer exists – it was bought by the Toohey brothers in 1873 and knocked down so they could build their Standard Brewery. But the Albion brewery lives on in street names in the Surry Hills area where it was located – names like Terry Street and Albion Street.

That placed it almost across the road from what is Central Station today. Back in the days of the brewery, though, it wasn't Central Station but a rather large cemetery. They dug up all the bodies there and relocated them before building Central over the top.

By some accounts it wasn't an especially nice place – for the living, that is. *The Illustrated Sydney News* in 1878 – in a piece calling for the government to do something about it – didn't think much of this "death-nest in our midst".

"If the money is sought to construct drains all round the ground to carry the essence of decayed humanity into the harbour sewers, or to remove the brick and stone buttress in Elizabeth Street, through which slimy and offensive matter oozes after rainy weather, and so somewhat lessen the evils likely to arise, we commend its probable appropriation as one more step forward."

You know where some of that "slimy and offensive matter" ended up? Yep, into the Albion Brewery beers. In a footnote to David Clark's essay on Sydney's water supply he mentions this rather unfortunate addition to Samuel Terry's beers.

"...Sydney's pollution problems are alleged to have actually improved the taste of the local beer. The Albion Brewery's water reservoir received the drainage from the Devonshire Street Cemetery and the beer it produced had a distinctive flavour, later found to be a product of the pollution."

Two things come to mind here. Firstly, that's disgusting. Secondly, if any footnote was ever worth expanding on, it's this one.

BIBLIOGRAPHY

So, here we are at the end of the book. Only the bibliography to go. But feel free to skip this part altogether, I won't blame you for a second. It's totally fine if you have something better to do.

You're still here? Well, you must be interested then. This bibliography exists for several reasons. Firstly, it's here to show you that I didn't make up all that stuff you just read; it all comes from a book, newspaper story, academic journal article, website or TV show. It's all accurate – at least as accurate as some guy who isn't a proper historian can make it.

Secondly, I included the bibliography as a way of avoiding the use of footnotes. Man, I hate footnotes. And only partially because the formatting of them is a real pain in the butt. They break the reader's flow because they have to stop every time they come across a tiny little number in the text and glance at the bottom of the page to see if it's anything important. And it's almost never anything important. Endnotes suck even harder; with them you have to keep flicking through to the back of the book to find out that looking was actually a total waste of time because all the note says is something like "Jenkins, op cit".

To get around the footnote/endnote thing, you may have noticed I've referred to books, journals or newspaper articles in the text. That was quite intentional; it means, if you're interested, you can check out the name of the person in the bibliography and find out where that information came from. You're on your own when it comes to a page number in the book, I couldn't be bothered going to that much trouble.

Thirdly, for those who are keen on finding out more about the history of beer in Australia, this can serve as a reading list. I've had to track down a lot of these works by reading the bibliographies of other books, by reading theses and academic journals and hammering Google. No reason for you to have to go and do all that again yourself. So you can enjoy the fruits of my book hunting.

And with that, I bid you good day, sir. Or lady.

Annear, Robyn, *Bearbrass – Imagining Early Melbourne*, Text Publishing, 2014
Atkinson, James, 'Biggest beer in Australia axed', *Australian Brews News*, May 5, 2015
Australian Bureau of Statistics, 'Apparent Consumption of Alcohol: Extended Time Series, 1944-45 to 2008-09, January 2011

Barry, Paul, 'How Alan Bond went bust in beer', *Beer and Brewer*, Autumn 2008.
Barry, Paul, *The Rise and Fall of Alan Bond*, ABC Books, 1990
Beveridge, Ann, 'How the booze bus changed pub culture', *The Daily Telegraph*, December 16, 2003
Beveridge, John, 'Is it time for a beer yet? Maybe Beefy nose', *The Herald Sun*, December 6, 2006
Beveridge, John, 'The mother of all beer ads', *The Herald Sun*, December 6, 2007
Bevilacqua, Simon, 'Boon's mo-tivation', *Sunday Tasmanian*, October 15, 2006

Birmingham, John, *Leviathan: The Unauthorised Biography of Sydney*, Knopf, 1999

Callister, Jamie, *The Man Who Invented Vegemite*, Pier 9, 2011
Cashmore, Judy, *The Impact of Random Breath Testing in NSW*, Attorney General's Department NSW Government, 1985
Clark, David 'Worse than Physic - Sydney's Water Supply 1788-1888' in Kelly, Max (ed), *Nineteenth-Century Sydney*, Sydney History Group, 1978
Cowie, Tom, 'Foster's super premium brew not so super', *Crikey*, September 21, 2010
Cusack, Dymphna and Edmonds, Catherine, *Caddie: The Autobiography of a Sydney Barmaid*, Angus & Robertson, 2015 (1953)
Cusack, Dymphna, and James, Florence, *Come In Spinner*, Angus and Robertson, 2013, (1951)

Darragh, Christie, 'Mosman's boy mascot company commander and the Valentine's Day mutiny', *Behind the Lines* website, February 14, 2016
Davis, Tony, 'Milestones: Breath testing goes random', *Sydney Morning Herald*, May 3, 2014
Deutsher, Keith M, *The Breweries of Australia*, Beer & Brewer Media, 2012
Dingle, AE, 'The Truly Magnificent Thirst – an historical survey of Australian drinking habits', *Historical Studies*, Volume 19, No 75, University of Melbourne, October 1980
Dunstan, Keith, *The Amber Nectar – A Celebration of Beer and Brewing in Australia*, Viking O'Neil, 1987
Duff, Eamonn, 'Found: Long-lost grave of Bennelong, *Sydney*

Morning Herald, March 20, 2011
Duff, Eamonn, 'Finding Bennelong', *Sunday Age*, March 27, 2011
Duff, Eamonn, Bennelong's remains too fragile to disturb', *Sun Herald*, September 18, 2011

Edmistone, Leone, 'Abduction deflates brewery staff', *Courier Mail*, June 23, 2004
England, Cameron, 'Coopers still a target in court Lion shot now for an aftermath', *The Advertiser*, December 17, 2005
Evans, Simon, 'Beer consumption at a 68-year low', *Australian Financial Review*, May 7, 2015
Evans, Simon, 'It's beers all round as the Boonanza takes hold', *Australian Financial Review*, February 18, 2006

Ferraz, Nalita, 'Fifteen years of blowing in the bag', *Illawarra Mercury*, December 17, 1997
Ferris, Jason, Devaney, Madonna, Sparkes-Carroll, Michelle and Davis, Gabbi, *A National Examination of Random Breath Testing and Alcohol-Related Traffic Crash Rates (2000-2012)*, Foundation for Alcohol Research and Education, March 2015
Fitzgibbon, Liam, 'Campo hits apology button after making a twit of himself', *Newcastle Herald*, September 11, 2013
Fitzgibbon, Liam, 'Team-mates not bitter at Ahmed ban on beer logo', *Sunday Mail*, September 8, 2013
Freeland, JM, *The Australian Pub*, Sun Books, 1977
Frith, Bryan, 'Sad day for shareholder rights as Coopers keeps in in family', *The Australian*, December 14, 2005
Fullagher, Kate, ''Bennelong in Britain, *Aboriginal History*, Volume 33, ANU Press

Gilling, Tom, *Grog – A Bottled History of Australia's First 30 Years*, Hachette Australia, 2016.
Greenblat, Eli, 'Coopers keeps it in the family', *The Age*, January 13, 2014

Hardy, Maggie and Schulz, Ben, 'Yes, you can make alcohol from Vegemite, but ...', *The Conversation*, August 14, 2015
Hasluck, Paul, *The Government and the People 1942-1945*, Australian War Memorial, 1970
Hawke, Bob, *The Hawke Memoirs*, William Heinemann, 1984
Hawthorne, Mark, 'If you hated Boonie, you've been Warned', *The Age*, December 7, 2007
Hinchcliffe, Jessica, 'We want beer: State Library of Queensland looking back at Brisbane's 1940 beer riots', ABC News website, April 11, 2015
Hill, Jennifer, Gibson, Elizabeth and Woodward, Theodora, *Heritage report for Halvorsen's Boat Yard*, Architectural Projects Ltd, August 7, 2014
Homel, Ross, 'Crime on the roads: drinking and driving' in *Alcohol and Crime*, Vernon, Julia (ed), Australian Institute of Criminology, 1990
Homel, Ross, 'Random breath testing and random stopping programs in Australia', in *Drinking and Driving: Advances in Research and Prevention*, Wilson, R Jean and Mann, Robert E (eds), Guildford Press, 1990
Horn, Allyson, 'Vegemite can be brewed into cheap form of beer, scientists say', *ABC News online*, August 15, 2016
Hunt, David, *Girt: The Unauthorised History of Australia*, Black Inc, 2013
Hughes, David, 'Australia's First Brewer', *Journal of the Royal*

Australian Historical Society, Volume 82, Part 2, December 1996
Hughes, Robert, *The Fatal Shore*, Vintage, 2003

James, Colin, 'How this stubby got the Coopers battle brewing', *Sunday Mail*, October 2, 2005
Jensen, Dr HI, 'The Darwin Rebellion', *Labour History*, November 1966

Karskens, Grace, *The Colony – A History of Early Sydney*, Allen & Unwin, 2009
Keneally, Thomas, *Australians – Origins to Eureka*, Allen & Unwin, 2009
Keneally, Thomas, *Australians – Eureka to the Diggers*, Allen & Unwin, 2011
Kirkegaard, Matt, 'Alan Bond and Bernie Power: Beer in the '80s', *Beer and Brewer*, Autumn 2008
Kingham, Ian, 'Real Brand Names Part 1', *Beer and Brewer*, Winter 2010
Kirkby, Diane Erica, 'Drinking 'The Good Life': Australia circa 1880-1980', *Alcohol: A Social and Cultural History*, edited by Mack P Holt, Berg, 2006
Kruger, John, 'Coopers Brewery – 150 years of beer and tradition', *Beer and Brewer*, Winter, 2012

Lalor, Peter, 'Drinking for Australia', *The Weekend Australian Magazine*, December 20, 2003
Lalor, Peter (editor), *Great Australian Beer Yarns*, ABC Books, 2014.
Laughland, Oliver, 'David Campese: Fawad Ahmed should 'go

home' if he won't wear beer logo', *The Guardian*, September 6, 2013

Leggett, Ben, 'The darker side of gin - mother's ruin', *Re: Magazine*, Spring 2015

Lehmann, John, 'Halal-earned thirst halts a big cold beer', *The Herald Sun*, September 6, 2013

Lewis, Milton, *A Rum State – Alcohol and State Policy in Australia 1788-1988*, Australian Government Publishing Service, 1992

Love, Simon, 'Vote out the Boroondara polls', *City Journal*, April 5, 2013

Luckins, Tanja, 'Pigs, Hogs and Aussie Blokes - the emergence of the term 'six o'clock swill', *History Australia*, Volume 4, Number 1, Monash University Press, 2007

Luckins, Tanya, 'Satan Finds Some Mischief: drinkers' response to the six o'clock closing of pubs in Australia', *Journal of Australian Studies*, Volume 32, Number 3, September, 2008

Maiden, Malcolm, 'Booney tunes', *The Age*, January 28, 2006

McDonald, Shae, 'Carlton and United Breweries Stops Regular Production of NT Draught', *NT News*, May 2, 2015

Meade, Kevin, 'Band feels a lawsuit coming on as Fourex joke falls flat', *The Australian*, December 11, 2004.

Media Watch, *Fermenting the Facts about Vegemite*, ABC TV, August 17, 2015

Milne, Chris, 'Fight weakens Coopers', *Australian Financial Review*, November 10, 2006

Moore, Tony, 'Vegemite builds beer, but not by itself: UQ researchers', *Brisbane Times*, August 15, 2016

Mundle, Rob, *The First Fleet*, ABC Books, 2014

Murgatroyd, Sarah, *The Dig Tree - The Story of Burke and Wills*, Text

Publishing, 2002

O'Keeffe, Kerry, *According to Skull: An Entertaining Stroll Through The Mind of Kerry O'Keeffe*, ABC Books, 2004.
Ockenden, Will, '30 Years of Random Breath Testing in NSW', *ABC Radio*, November 20, 2012
Oliver, Garrett (ed), *The Oxford Companion to Beer*, Oxford University Press, 2012

Painter, Alison, Cooper, Tim and Linn, Rob, *Jolly Good Ale and Old – Coopers Brewery 1862-2012*, Coopers Brewery, 2013
Parnell, Sean and Hogg, Marie, 'Drinks down as Aussies cringe at the binge, *The Australian*, May 7, 2015
Partridge, Emma, 'Baird says VB logo is just not cricket', *Newcastle Herald*, September 18, 2013
Pearl, Cyril, *Beer, Glorious Beer*, Thomas Nelson, 1969
Phillips, Walter, 'Six O'Clock Swill – the introduction of early closing of hotel bars in Australia', *Historical Studies*, Volume 19, Number 75, University of Melbourne, October 1980.

Reinecke, Carl, 'The Other Charge of the Light Brigade', *Griffith Review 28*, May 2010.
Richardson, Nick, 'A tale of two Boonys', *The Herald Sun*, February 17, 2006
Russell, Christopher, 'Beer wars begin amicably', *The Herald Sun*, November 30, 2015
Rose, Ian, 'The dry zone', *The Age*, January 25, 2013
Ryan, Chris, 'The Battle of Central Station', *Sydney Outsider*, April

18, 2014

Saltau, Chloe, 'David Campese tells Fawad Ahmed to 'go home'over VB logo ban', *Sydney Morning Herald*, September 6, 2013.
Saltau, Chloe, 'Foster's regrets binge-drinking Boonie figurine', *Sydney Morning Herald*, October 30, 2009
Simpson, Willie, 'There are those who say neigh', *Sydney Morning Herald*, August 10, 2010
Smith, Bridie, 'Boony's shout – it just won't go away', *The Age*, May 9, 2006
Smith, Keith Vincent, 'Bennelong among his people', *Aboriginal History*, Volume 33, ANU Press
Stevenson, Andrew, 'A long and bumpy road to RBT', *Sydney Morning Herald*, December 17, 2012
Straw, Leigh, *The Worst Woman in Sydney: The Life and Crimes of Kate Leigh*, NewSouth Publishing, 2016
Stubbs, Brett J, 'A New Drink for Young Australia: from ale to lager beer in New South Wales, 1880 to 1930', *Food, Power and Community*, edited by Robert Dare, Wakefield Press, 1999
Stubbs, Brett J, 'Beer and War in Australia', *Australian Brews News* website, July, 2012
Stubbs, Brett J, *Beer, Mines and Rails: A history of the brewing industry in Queensland to the 1920s*, Tankard Books, 2010
Stubbs, Brett J, 'Captain Cook's Beer; the antiscorbutic use of malt and beer in late 18th century sea voyages', *Asia Pacific Journal of Clinical Nutrition*, February 2003
Stubbs, Brett J, *Very Good Beer and Ale: Breweries and Brewers of Tasmania 1820s to 1930s*, Tankard Books, 2013
Sturma, Michael, *Vice in a Vicious Society: Crime and Convicts in Mid*

19th Century NSW, University of Queensland Press, 1983
Sygal, David, 'Muslim spinner given leave to keep a sponsor off his back', *Sydney Morning Herald*, September 13, 2013
Symons, Michael, *One Continuous Picnic: A Gastronomic History of Australia*, Melbourne University Press, 2007
Symons, Peter, *Bronzed Brews: Home Brewing Old Australian Beers*, Tritun, 2015

Thoeming, J Peter, *Here's Too'ee: The Story of Tooheys*, Crawford House Publishing
Topsfield, Jewel, 'Sober Camberwell to vote on Indian drought, *The Age*, April 9, 2005
Tucker, Jim, 'Beefy and Boony are cut down to size', *Courier Mail*, November 22, 2006

Unknown, 'Cache of Liquor forfeited', *Canberra Times*, May 25, 1943
Unknown, 'Camberwell diners can raise their glasses', *The Age*, May 15, 2015
Unknown, 'Campese sorry for Ahmed comment', *The Age*, September 11, 2013
Unknown, 'Charges of mutiny', *Sydney Morning Herald*, March 28, 1916
Unknown, 'Colonial Loyalty at Toorak', *The Melbourne Age*, June 5, 1855
Unknown, 'Crack open your Boony', *MX*, January 13, 2006
Unknown, 'Drinking and driving do not mix', *Illawarra Mercury*, October 31, 1950
Unknown, *James Squire/s – The Remarkable Life of Australia's First Brewer*, Fellowship of First Fleeters – Hunter Valley chapter

website

Unknown, 'James Sutherland lashes out at racist abuse of Fawad Ahmed', *cricketcountry.com website*, September 4, 2013

Unknown, 'Liquid gold reward offered', *Courier Mail*, December 23 2005

Unknown, 'Magic Mo-ment', *Hobart Mercury*, November 16, 2005

Unknown, 'Mr Edmund Resch permitted to leave camp', *Sydney Morning Herald*, March 1, 1918

Unknown, 'Mr Fourex found lying in a ditch', *Sydney Morning Herald*, June 24, 2004

Unknown, 'Our drinking habits badly needed civilising', *Sydney Morning Herald*, November 8, 1945

Unknown, 'Prohibition in Canberra: King O'Malley and the 'Dry' Capital', *Your Memento Issue 10*, National Archives of Australia, April 2013.

Unknown, 'Six o'clock swill', *Perth Daily News*, October 4, 1944

Unknown, 'Soldiers refuse to drill', *Sydney Morning Herald*, February 15, 1916

Unknown, 'Soldiers' Riot', *Kalgoorlie Western Argus*, February 29, 1916

Unknown, 'Sydney brewer interned - Mr Edmund Resch', *Sydney Morning Herald*, November 27, 1917

Unknown, 'Talking Boonie', *Mr Speaker* website, www.mrspeaker.net

Unknown, 'The internment of Edmund Resch', *Barrier Miner* (Broken Hill), December 3, 1917

Unknown, 'The Liverpool mutiny – inquest on a soldier', *Hobart Mercury*, March 1, 1916

Unknown, 'The mutiny – Trooper Keefe's death', *Sydney Morning Herald*, March 1, 1916

Unknown, 'Warnie into bat as Boonie retires', *Launceston*

Examiner, October 3, 2007
Unknown, 'Where's ya mo, Beefy?', *MX*, November 22, 2006

Verity, William, 'Driving force', *Illawarra Mercury*, December 1, 2007

Welborn, Suzanne, *Swan: The History of a Brewery*, University of Western Australia Press, 1987
White, John, *Journal of a Voyage to New South Wales*, 1790
Wilkinson, John, *Alcohol and Tobacco in NSW: Consumption, Revenue and Concern*, NSW Parliamentary Library Research Service, 1997
Wilson, David, 'Pricey pint: how I developed the world's most expensive ale', *Sydney Morning Herald*, November 30, 2010
Wray, Michael, 'XXXX marks the spot of icon's disappearance', *Courier Mail*, December 21, 2005.
Writer, Larry, *Razor: Tilly Devine, Kate Leigh and the Razor Gangs*, Pan Macmillan, 2001

Index

Abbott, Tony, a wuss for drinking a middie, 6
Alice Springs Brewery 88
Anderson, Robert 18
Annear, Robyn 8
Australia, apparent lack of research into before First Fleet's arrival 22-23
Australia Day and beer 25-26

Banks, Joseph 22-24
Barrett, Thomas 35-38
Batmobile 185
Battle of Central Station 101-107
Beer brewing on the First Fleet 27
Beer is better than rum 61, 88
Beer Is Your Friend website, free plugging thereof 2
Beer rankings 11-12
Benaud, Richie, people at the cricket dressed up as 6
Bennelong 50-57
Bennelong Point 43-44
The Benny Hill Show theme song 24
Bible, how to explain away all those alcohol references 114
Bigge Inquiry 42
Bjekle-Petersen, Joh 147, 160
Boag, James 92-93
Boag's 87
Boggs, Wade 169-170

Bombala – almost the nation's capital 98
Bond, Alan 91, 94, 171-177
Bond Brewing 174-175
Boon, David 6, 167-170, 183-190
Boony or Boonie? 7
Boroondara 118-119
Boston, John 7, 39-42
Botany Bay 23-24, 26
Botham, Ian 187-188
Bougainville, Louis-Antoine de 15
Bowes Smyth, Arthur 27-30, 37
Brettanomyces 194
Brew Dog 192
Brooks, Captain John 15
Bruntnell, Albert 125
BWS 40

Caddie 128-129
Canadian Club 183
Canberra, jokes about how boring it is 95
Canberra, no beer in town 96-100
Canning Affair, The 46-48
Canning, Elizabeth, 46-48
Capsicum as a weird ingredient in beer 71
Cascade 87
Cascade Brewery 92
Castlemaine Perkins 144-145, 174-176
Cauliflower, not even a First Fleet convict will steal it 31
Carlton and United 6, 149-153, 175, 180-182, 193-195

Carlton and United miss the boat on Vegemite 138
Central Station riot 1, 2, 101-107
Champagne, Melbourne totally goes mad for 8
Charlotte 24-25, 35, 42, 45
Chicken theft 44
Clark, Manning 28-30
Clark Ralph 29
Cleeves Park 55-56
Coates, Denis 103
Coffee palaces 113-114
Colbee 51
Cole, EW 114-116
Collins, David 52-53
Colonial twang 9, 70
Come In Spinner 129
Cook, Captain James 15-20, 22-23
Cooper, Ann 68-69
Cooper, Thomas 68-72, 179, 182
Cooper, Dr Tim 93, 180
Coopers 67-72, 93, 179-182
Cozens, John 194-195
Crocker, Barry 84
Crocodiles 150
Crown Ambassador 193-195
Cubex 138, 140
Curtin, John 129
Cusack, Dymphna 128-129

Daedalus 42
Dampier, William 15

Dan Murphy's 40
Dartboards, say goodbye to them 122
Darwin Rebellion 2, 131-136
Darwin residents get riled up 134-136
Darwin Stubby 149-153
Dead Marines 8
Devonshire Street Cemetery 57
Diarrhea caused by bad beer 71
Dingle, AE 8
Dodgy maths about the size of beer barrels on *The Endeavour* 17-18
Donkey Kong, it's on like 125
Dr Tim's 93
Drinking a crapload of beers 6
Drinking rates 8-13
Drost, Mary 119
Drunken rootfest of the First Fleet, allegations of 27-30
Duff, Eamon 56
Dwarf was the inspiration for Mr Fourex 146

Eagle Blue 180
Early brewing efforts 9, 26
Eccles, Thomas 31
Eureka Stockade 131
Emu Bitter 93-94
Endeavour 15-20

Fairstar the Funship 17
Farnell, James Squire 46
Ferdinand, Franz (not the band) 1

Fiftyy-two cans 166-170
First Fleet 2, 7, 20, 21-30, 33, 35, 42, 45
Furphy's Refreshing Ale 91
Forging money while on the First Fleet 36
Forrest, John 98
Foster, William and Ralph 82-84
Foster's 81-85, 176
Foster's Brewery, but not the one you're thinking of 88
Foundational orgy 27-31
Four 'Wives' 50
Fourex condoms 147-148
Friendship 24
"Fuck off Boony" 187-188

G Heilemann Brewing Company 177
Gallipoli 102, 106
Gargantuan pissheads 17
Gascoyne, Sir Crisp 47
George Patterson Y&R 184-186
Gilruth, John 133-136
Gin, British go absolutely mad for 61-62
Gold Rush 123
Going to jail for being German 76-79
Great Depression 9
Great Expectations used as a metaphor even though I haven't read it 74
Green, Alexander 34

Hahn, Chuck 40

Hall, Joseph 36-37
Hanging 33-38
Hangman pale ale 34
Harts Pub 34, 35, 38
Hawke, Bob 6
Headhunters eat Australia's second brewer 44
Hogan, Paul 81, 84
Hogarth, William 61-62
Holman, William 125
Horizontal fraternisation, an overwrought way of saying "sex" 30
Horne, Donald iii, 12
Hotham, Sir Charles, party is a total bust 70-71
Hughes, Robert 42
Hughes Merv
Hunt, David 1

Ice as a marketing ploy to sell beer 83

Jackson, Wayne 180-181
Jeez, *The Endeavour* was a really small ship 16
Johnnie Walker 123
Jones, Dean 167

Kansas, where a federal politician was really born 96
Karskens, Grace 28-29
KB 90
Keefe, Ernest William 103, 106-107
King George III 50
King O'Malley's, totally ironic name for Canberra pub 100
King, Philip Gidley 25-26, 60-63

Kirin 11, 12, 91, 181
Kirkegaard, Matt 174-175
Kirkby, Diane 10
Kissing Point 45

Lady Penrhyn 24, 27-29
Lavell, Henry 36-37
Lawson, Geoff 167
Leigh, Kate 123
Low-alcohol beer 162-163
Lillee, Dennis 167
Lion Nathan 50, 93, 180-182
Little Creatures 91
Local option laws 116-119
Logan, Marcus 105-107
Love-apple, which is a bloody stupid name for a tomato if you ask me 41-42

Malt Shovel Brewery 40
Malting Shovel 40
Matilda Bay 152
Man with the weird first name of Crisp 47
Manly Cove 52
Marsh, Rodney 166-167
McAlister, Cyril 139-140
McKenzie, Barry 84
Miller Lite 169
Mitchell, Peter 56-57
Moonshine 142
Mr Fourex 145-147

Murphy's swipes 70-71
Myth of the Australian beer drinker 12-13

Nachos 185
Nail Antarctic Pale Ale 192-193
Nail Brewing 192-193
Nelson, Harold
NT Draught 87, 94, 151-153

O'Malley, King 95-100
Oddy, James, one of those brewers who drowned in a vat of beer
One Fifty Lashes 50
O'Keeffe, Kerry 166
Orton, Richard, sailor who had his ears chopped off while drunk 18

Paciullo, George 159-161
Paddington frisk 34
Parwill 140
Passive-aggressive corporate fight 41
Perouse, Comte de la 24
Phillip, Governor Arthur 7, 21-24, 52-53
Porter 7, 25-26
Power, Bernie 90-91, 174-175
Powers Brewing 91
Pride of Ringwood joke 45
Prince of Wales 24
Princip, Gavrilo, totally show-off reference to, 1

Queanbeyan, where Canberrans went to get drunk 99-100

Random Breath Testing 157-163
Reading, John, killed by alcohol 18
Resch, Edmund 73-79, 90
Resch, Emil 78-79
Resch's 73, 74, 87, 90, 91, 123, 172, 176
Reverse Boonjaneering 190
Rocks Brewing Company 34
Rubbish attempt by the First Fleet to play it cool when leaving Botany Bay 24
Rum 7
Rum Rebellion that wasn't really about rum 60-61, 132
Rushton, Thomas 63
Ryan, John 36-37

Sanity prevails and six o'clock closing ends 126
Sailors drinking beer too fast on *The Endeavour* 17
Sailors getting totally drunk on *The Endeavour* 18
Sailors being so drunk they don't realise someone is cutting off their ears 18
Scullion, Nigel 141
Scurvy 19-20
Sea Shepherd 193
Second Fleet 43
Sever, William Crompton 24
Simpson, Bob 168
Simpson, Willie 194
Six Foot Hick 147
Six o'clock closing 9, 107, 112, 117, 121-130
Six o'clock rush 127-129
Six o'clock swill 10, 127-129
Skase, Christopher 171

Spakfilla 2
Speechifying 96
Squire, James 7, 39-41, 42-46, 50, 51, 52-55
Squires, Mary 47-48
Stallwood, John, 192-193
Stagger juice 97
Stubbs, Brett J 8, 19, 79
Supply 25
Surprize 41
Swan Brewery 173
Sydney Cove 25-30
Sydney Gazette's brutal obituary for Bennelong 55
Sydney Harbour, can you believe Captain Cook missed it? 24
Sydney Opera House 53

Talking Boony Dolls 183-190
Temperance movement in Australia 107, 111-130
Tench, Watkin 29, 51
The Constable 40, 50
The End of History 192
The Evils of Drink Traffic, long but entertaining quote from 115-116
The Fatal Shore 42
The King, Bennelong's name for wine 51
The Rocks 34, 38
The Swindler 50
Toohey's Brewery 104, 175-176
Toohey, John Thomas and James, 74
Tooth and Co 90, 123, 140
Totem Tennis 185

Van Gogh, Vincent, cheap joke at the expense of 19
Vaz de Torres, Luis 15
Vegemite 137-142
Vegemite, can you make booze out of it? 141-142
Venezuela, a country that drinks more beer that us (surprising, huh?) 12
Vesteys 133-134
Victoria Bitter 6, 81, 87, 89, 91, 151, 169, 172, 183-190
Vincent Smith, Keith 52
Volstead Act 117
Voltron 185

Waterhouse, Henry 52-53
Walker, Fred 139-140
Walters Doug 166-167, 169
Warne, Shane 188
Wattle Pale Ale and other beers once made by Foster's Brewing Company 84
Waverly Brewery that isn't actually in Waverly 75
Wells, Susannah 47
West End Brewery 93
Wet horse blanket 194
White, John 36
Wine 11
Wine Society 40
Women's Christian Temperance Union 113
Woolworths 40
World record for drinking a Darwin Stubby 151-152
World War I 34, 76-77, 121, 124, 127, 128
World War II 10, 128, 130

Wort 19
Wran, Neville 161

XXXX 81, 87, 89, 143-148

Yemmerawamme, 53

The Slab

Sometimes at the very end of a movie, after the credits roll, there's a short scene that rewards those who hang around. Not many people do that; these days, credits take so long because it seems anyone who so much as walked past the set while they were filming gets a mention. Only those with nothing better to do with their time are going to sit in the cinema seat while the credits roll, just on the off chance there's an amusing coda right at the end.

The creation of DVDs and pay TV made it so much easier to check the end for these scenes. Now, at the end of every film I watch at home I fast-forward through the credits to see if there is a little surprise at the end. Which annoys my wife more than a little bit. Though not as much as the fact that my daughter now insists on checking the end of her movies too.

What's this got to do with a book about beer? Well, I'm doing the book version of that extra scene at the end, the one that rewards those who stick around. So here's one last beer story, about a week where some people went nuts because a cricketer didn't want to wear a beer logo.

The cricketer in question was Fawad Ahmed, a leg-spinner who was born in Pakistan. He arrived in Australia in 2010 on a short-stay visa but then applied for refugee status, claiming persecution by religious extremists. He was eventually granted permanent residency in November 2012 and, later that month, signed with the Melbourne Regenades in the Big Bash League.

In July 2013 he was granted Australian citizenship, and made his national T20 debut in August of that year. He was picked for the One-Day International series against England the following month, which is when the week-long furore began.

A devout Muslim, Ahmed had issues with the logo for VB – a team sponsor – appearing on his shirt. Discussions were had with Ahmed, Cricket Australia and CUB, with the result that he could wear an unbranded shirt.

"Cricket Australia and Carlton and United Breweries are respectful of Fawad's personal beliefs and have agreed with his request to wear an unbranded shirt," Cricket Australia executive general manager of operations Mike McKenna said.

"CUB have been a long-standing partner of Australian cricket for more than 17 years and Fawad was thankful for their understanding of his personal situation."

And there it should have ended, but for the outpouring of what Cricket Australia CEO James Sutherland called "racist comments" on social media. "Legitimate reason RELIGION, not it's not, it's a game of cricket, not praying at a church," said one tweet.

"It is driven by money and fans not by religious fanatics. Those who don't like the Australian culture should leave, or keep misguided values to themselves."

Perhaps, like me, you're wondering what wearing a VB logo has to do with "Australian culture". Everything kicked up a notch when some former sportsmen opened their mouths.

One was Doug Walters, a former Test cricketer and beer lover (he set the beer drinking record David Boon would break. Ahem, *allegedly*). Walters didn't like the special treatment Ahmed got.

"I think if he doesn't want to wear the team gear, he should not be part of the team," Walters said. "Maybe if he doesn't want to be paid, that's OK."

The Slab

Former rugby union international David Campese doubled down, with a "go back to where you came from" tweet. Which never makes a person look good.

"Doug Walters tells Pakistan-born Fawad Ahmed: if you don't like the VB uniform, don't play for Australia. Well said Doug. Tell him to go home," Campese tweeted.

He didn't back down in follow-up tweets prompted by his initial outburst either. Here's a sample of a few as reported in the *Sydney Morning Herald*, complete with punctuation errors.

"well why did he come to Aussie for in the first place. A better life? Now he is telling people what he wants.!"

"It is not about religion it is about sport. I don't care about what he believes. It is about sport. That's all."

"I played under the XXXX logo. Played. I didn't drink beer! He came to Australia for a better life?"

"we were supported by XXXX and I was not a beer drinker. So Doug is right go back to where you came from."

Again, it is worth remembering, this whole thing is about the logo of a beer company. Ahmed said nothing negative about Australia or Australians, and yet some people – Campese included – threw all the toys out of the cot and somehow equated a quietly-stated desire not to wear a beer logo with giving Australia a slap in the face.

Perhaps realising his rants had done himself no favours, Campese apologised on Twitter. At least it was called an apology in the media – after reading the relevant tweets, I'm not so sure it was.

"Just like to say sorry for a comments [sic]," he tweeted. "It is about sport and never had or will be about religion. Any man who knows me can tell you that. I will be ringing the ACA to say sorry and to pass my message on. Sport is about team work and team. That was my point. Sorry again."

See what I mean? I'm not even sure Campese knew what was wrong about his comments in the first place. Where's the apology for his "go back to where you came from" remarks? Where's the acknowledgement that Ahmed's own team-mates said they couldn't care less what shirt he wore?

One can't help but wonder if the same furore would have arisen if the sponsor's logo Ahmed declined to wear had been a bank's and not a beer brand. I'd suggest not because, while the reality is very different, some Aussies still really see beer as part of the Australian identity. Therefore, to them, disrespecting beer is akin to disrespecting the Australian way of life.

www.ingramcontent.com/pod-product-compliance
Lightning Source LLC
Chambersburg PA
CBHW031413290426
44110CB00011B/362